WHAT
IS
MAN

*A Definitive Explanation of the Origins and
Creation of Man*

Dray Scott

KP PUBLISHING COMPANY

ISBN: 978-1-950936-25-0 (Paperback)
ISBN: 978-1-950936-26-7 (Ebook)
Library of Congress Control Number: Pending

Editor: Martha Tucker
Cover Design: Angie Alaya
Literary Director: Sandra L. Slayton

Published by KP Publishing
Valencia, CA 91355
www.kp-pub.com
www.knowledgepowerinc.com

Printed in the United States of America

MANDATES

WHO I AM
Dray Scott

At times I thought I knew everything,
just to find out in time, I knew nothing.

Who am I? What am I? Why am I? How am I?

I heard some say, love yourself, how am I to love myself
when the self I am to love, I don't even know.

My Heavenly Father, Whatever I am, whoever I am,
why I am, I may not know, but I know I am yours.

All I have you gave me.
All I know you taught me.
Whatever I am you sustain me to be.
As far as I can see,

I am one with thee,
the unknowable, invisible eternity.

INTRODUCTION

The goal of the author is to bring down the truth from its lofty abstractness as it is disguised in religious and philosophical settings. This book aims to take the truth of who man is, and through this redemptive revelatory knowledge, the reader is empowered to regain his identity and self-respect.

Not all, but most people recognize that Man is a triune being made up of three parts: spirit, soul, and body. Yet, what is not so clear is how these three parts operate independently. Still, what is even less obvious to most is how to understand, work with, and harmonize these separate units of their whole being. History shows us that we have had a better grasp of the manifested material aspect of the world, but a clouded view of the invisible spiritual aspects of our being. We wander in the world like lost souls with no spiritual direction trying to find a religion or spiritual practice that will suit us. Many of us neglect the spiritual aspect of our being; thus, catering to the flesh with the pleasures of the world.

Furthermore, we study western and eastern psychology and try to apply their ever-evolving science of mind which becomes increasingly confusing as a result of the new theories that come with them. We claim to have the best healthcare to cure different diseases, but we don't care for our health at all, we manage disease and practice medicine.

Mental health issues are growing at a fast pace, and scientists don't know if it's a growing epidemic or something that has been here undiscovered for a while. Yet from a material perspective, we create, invent, and use advanced technologies in such a progressive manner that a year-old product is obsolete. We need to balance ourselves spiritually, mentally, and physically. As you read this book, you will discover why all of these are essential to life, peace and being in one accord with ourselves in a holistic manner.

What we will discuss in this book *WHAT IS MAN?* is the creation of Man by Yahweh its Creator according to the Bible, how Man was created, where he was created, and what Man's responsibility is to his creation and Creator is. We will also take a detailed look at Man's opposition to fulfilling this responsibility, by taking note of his adversary. We will also take a detailed look at "Existence and Life," "Duality and Oneness," "Being Spiritual," "Self-identity," "Satan and his Works," "The Mind over Material," and "The Kingdom of Heaven" to name a few.

What is Man? is written in three parts: Man's Identity, Man's Dominion, and Man's Accuser or Opposition, and then a final concluding chapter that culminates on a close look at The Messiah (Son of YHWH Son of Man). The book contains chapters; however, they will be referred to as mandates as they confer the mindset of the kingdom language from our King and Creator. At the end of each mandate or chapter, you will get a sense of responsibility and empowerment to master and apply what is taught and learned.

You will find that the book is written with the conviction that all opposition can be overcome by applying the right knowledge to any problem. I want to encourage the reader to be in charge of his or her divine purpose and existence.

The author aims to convey to every reader the knowledge needed to do this. Hence, the purpose of this book is to be a tool for the reader to gain a deep understanding, and the ability to maximize his or her potentials here on earth as an individual of a divine origin and purpose. It is the author's opinion that if you gain the knowledge of self, you will relate to the world around you in a more positive and responsible manner; you will be inclined to take your rightful place in the earth, having the dominion you were created to have, and you will be able to overcome anything from sickness to heartbreak, from low self-esteem to poverty, and ultimately overcome death itself. To emancipate the soul of humanity is the goal of all the spiritual leaders of the present and past and the Holy books out of which they teach. There can be no lasting opposition to wisdom, knowledge, and understanding. It is your divine right to live a full, balanced, and abundant life and overcome any opposition to your prosperity and fruitfulness. It is the author's hope that you will gain the insight and courage through this work to mount those endeavors and ride into the golden sunset of your life and never be dominated again but have dominion and be fruitful for the remainder of your existence here on Earth.

If you are an atheist or agnostic, I ask that you tolerate the language of this book and see to the principles presented in it. I'm sure you will find ample evidence to the truths held herein that doesn't require faith in any God or religion to see.

With humility and honesty, it is my honor to present *What Is Man?*

MAN'S IDENTITY

- The creation of Man
- The existence of Man (male and female); Indivisible duality
- The Triunity and make up of man
- The science of naming

MANDATE I
The Creation of Man

Written stories about creation were obtained from the oral traditions worldwide. These stories were passed down verbally from one generation to the next, ofttimes coded with symbolism. The Sumerian and Cushite (Black African) text and traditions, where it is believed that the Bible gets most of its accounts from, is taken into consideration as I recount the biblical tales. For the purpose of this work, I use the well-known Christian version of the Bible (NKJ), which was derived from the Aramaic, Hebrew and Greek manuscripts. Since this is not a historical work, we do not need to concern ourselves with which Bible is first or more original but only with the facts of creation, which all the holy writings attest to. For the sake of this book, we will sharpen our focus on the fact that man was created and has an identity that traces back to the Creator in whose image and likeness man was created.

WHAT IS MAN?

The Bible narrates as follows:

Bersheet 1:1-2 (Genesis 1:1-2) In the beginning Elohim created the heavens and the earth. 2: The earth was without form, and void; and darkness was on the face of the deep. And the Spirit of YHWH was hovering over the face of the waters. 3: Then Elohim said, "Let there be light"; and there was light. 4: And Elohim saw the light that it was good; and Elohim divided the light from the darkness. First, I wish to direct the reader's attention to the Hebrew word for create which is "Bara." Bara deals with more of a thought or a contemplation rather than the idea of making something; this will become relevant when we talk about Man and the world(s) he exists in. You may be saying, "Hold on, the worlds man exists in? I thought it was only one world." Yet, we say phrases like the following all the time: "That was out of this world!" "So what world was it in?" "You must be out of your natural mind." "Is there a supernatural or other than natural mind to be in?" We say things like, "She passed out or was knocked out." And so on. What did she pass out into or what was she knocked out of consciousness into? We must know intuitively or at least subconsciously that we exist in other worlds or mental states of awareness as well as in this so called normal one we are conscious of. All things began at the beginning, so in this mandate, we will take a close look at the creation of Man and his Creator who he is a reflection of. Let's start by looking at *Ha Sefer Bereshit* 1:26 (The book of Genesis 1:26) 26: Then *Yahweh* said, "Let us make humans in our image, in our likeness. Let them rule the fish in the sea, the birds in the sky, the domestic animals all over the earth, and all the animals that crawl on the earth." 27: So *Elohim* created humans in his image. In the image of *Elohim* he created them. He created them male and female. 28: *Yahweh* blessed them and said, "Be fertile, increase in number, fill the earth, and be its master. Rule the fish in the sea, the birds in the sky, and all the animals that crawl on the earth." 29: *Elohim* said, "I have given you every plant with seeds on the face of the earth and every tree that has fruit with seeds. This will be your food. 30: I have given all green plants as food to every land animal, every bird in the sky, and every animal that crawls on the earth—every living, breathing animal." And so it was. 31: And *Elohim* saw everything that he had made and that it was very good. There was evening, then morning—the sixth day.

I will explain from these verses of the Scripture how involution precedes evolution and then that there was an execution of that which was decided upon. In other words, a thought and desire were first, next is an expression of that thought, then a performance of that thought; then a full manifestation of that performance is the sequence of events laid before us. We will not explore in-depth who the "us" may be as the plural word "*Elohim*" implies more than one; it will at this point suffice us to know that Man was created. It is however important that we discuss the nature and makeup of the Being in whose image and likeness Man was created in- as it will help us to identify who, why, and what we are as Man.

WHAT IS MAN?

We should see from the Scripture that the place of Man's creation is on a fully developed and inhabited Earth, which implies that man's Creator, is thoughtful - and thoughtfulness implies care and concern. We should also take note of the fact that Man's relationship to the Creator is implied by the importance of the position and responsibility that the Creator gives to him. He made Man fewer in number than all other created things and even with multiplying as a race, all other things multiply also. Like all rare and valuable things, the fewer in number created the greater the value rises for the owner. Also, it is important for several reasons to understand that the planet was designed perfectly that no matter how the population grows there would never be a shortage of food or resources. His intent to make man the ruler over all the earth is emphatic and of a major importance. It is no wonder why the Master is referred to as both the Creator and the Heavenly Father. On first sight, you can see that this is none other than a relationship between a father and his children inheriting and receiving the gift of dominion over the work of His great creation. There is one more thing that the text indicates about the Creator and that is growth, increase, multiplication, and replenishing, is His mode of operation. What does that mean? Well for one thing, everything that does not follow this mode is evidently not of His origin.

Secondly, it shows His progressive intent for creation to evolve and revolve which is the entire creative process, involution, evolution, and revolution. Here, we see a threefold operation designed by the Creator and it is replete throughout all His creation. The Creator's ideas are grandiose, and He thinks greatly—look at the complex galaxies and gigantic planets in it. He harnesses power with grace and thinks expansively–just look at lightning, electromagnetism, Toroidal Vortexes, black holes, light, dark and anti-matter, wormholes, and so on. The sciences of our times are tracing His steps trying to find His face as the "Grand Architect" and those in opposition of this "Intelligent designer of the cosmos" are out to prove that nothing brought forth everything; yet, the thing in discussion is of such importance to man that the enigma must be sought out. I suggest humbly that His signature is on everything including the man in search of it all.

There are a plethora of books that teach the creation story. So, I would love you to follow me on a journey to uncover more hidden aspects of this text and not just deal with the surface of the text. There are three keys we need to unlock the treasure chest of jewels these Scriptures contain: the Hebrew word for create (Bara), the words imagination (*Yetser*) and likeness (*Tselem*), the Male and Female dynamic.

The Hebrew word Bara is the word create, which is the spiritual act of emanating a desire from the heart and forming it in the mind. Meanwhile, the Spirit is the state of undifferentiated energy before it passes into form or matter. An act of creation is what we can better define as involution; *an act or instance of involving or entangling; the state of being involved, formulating something complicated.* This word also shows us that the Creator feels, thinks, and consciously formulates a plan of action within Himself. You will see each word as it relates to Man's creation like the words **form** (*Yetzirah*) and **made** (*Asiah*) converge and emerge from and into one another. This will become more important when we discuss later–the worlds in which man exists. The Creator first takes on the complicated task of creating (from beginning to end) man's potential, purpose, and nature of existence.

His motivation is self-expression born out of self-love and the desire to share the power of life from that self-love. He bestows on man a high honor by making man after the pattern of His own omniscient mind to reflect Him on earth as He is in the Heavens or the Spiritual realm. It is herein important to note that creation is the self-expression of the Spirit of The Infinite Eternal Creator that evolves and takes on various forms. Yet, all the varieties in secondary action are from one mind and one source no matter how varied. The eternally subsisting One must move into a dual existing form of energy and substance (known in electrical work as polarity) to create or form the world. Polarity creates a circuit as energy passes between the two opposite points; this circuit creates a unit of power. This should safeguard us from concluding that *YHWH* separates or divides Himself. Apparent duality is merely a way of self-expression, as we can safely assume that energy can only be known by reason of something that is energized, so must the creator be known by what is created. When we consider the Hebrew word *Echad* (one) as it is used in the Scripture in explaining that *YHWH* is One (Deuteronomy 6:4), we could describe this oneness as a unit. When it is seen that *Yahweh Eloa* is a UNIT then it is easier to understand how one essence can manifest in different forms just as energy does. The law of physics states that all energy is constant but just changes form. A unit can be an inseparable component as with all irreducibly complex things. If you take one part from the other, then it ceases to be. It is clearly seen how *YHWH* is one when you look at His attributes.

Theology teaches that *YHWH* is omniscient, well we must ask, if He is all knowing then there must be something to be known? If He is omnipresent, at all places, absent from nowhere, then there must be a somewhere for His presence to be. How do we know that force is being used unless it is used on something? How do we know that something is being said unless someone is conscious and present to hear or see? So, this oneness or unit that *YHWH* is has everything to do with creation. Though He does not need creation to possess His being, He does need creation to express His being. He could not be manifested as a Spirit if there is nothing and no one to make Himself known to. He is one with all that He creates and if creation ceases to be then *YHWH* ceases to exist as Spirit, and this is why the Scriptures opened up that in the beginning *Elohim* (plural) created.

The plural of the word *"Elohim"* is *YHWH* and the phrase "let us make man in our image" is of no bewilderment when understood from this paradigm. The Bible makes it clear as does most of the ancient writings that the oneness and unity of the Creator is key to understanding all of creation. The All Originating power is "in essence" unity "in manifestation" multiplicity. From one Mind came all, so man and all creation are a product of that one mind which unifies us in what we call a universe (unit = one, Verse = versatility or variation). In other words, energy and substance. This word substance should give clue to what I'm trying to convey for the prefix sub means under or below and the word stance can be described as abiding or manifested reality.

The Merriam-Webster dictionary defines substance as a particular kind of matter with uniform properties. The real physical matter of which a person or thing consists and which has a tangible, solid presence.

> *The Bible in Hebrews 11:1, tells us, "Now faith is the substance of things hoped for, the evidence of things not seen. 3: Through faith, we understand that the worlds were framed by the word of God so that things which are seen were not made of things which do appear.*

Energy and substance, Heaven and Earth, particles and waves, male and female, cause and effect, are all opposite ends of the same thing.

Let us take a look at the words image and likeness as they are used in the creation narrative.

Image or imagination is the Hebrew word **Yetser** (a *form, framing, purpose, or intent*). Yetser = Mental.

The word likeness is closely related and is the Hebrew word **Tselem** *(a pattern, design, or cut out).* Tselem = Substance.

What comes to the mind when you see the definitions to these words? One would be correct if the thoughts of quantity and quality come up. If you've imaged mathematics and geometry with **Yetser** and blueprint or model with **Tselem** then your thinking is in line with the concept of the biblical text. Not simply the math and geometry you learned in grade school, but chemistry and that of scientific discovery like Nanos, subatomic and atomic particles, solids, gas, liquids and plasma, DNA, RNA, ATP, protein molecules, minerals, and monatomic elements, etc.

What of the blueprint or model? Well, let's explore that. The text answers the question when it says, "Male and Female are what he made man to be after His likeness." If this is true, then we should be able to substantiate the trueness of it by examining the material world and man that is made of it. Every other thing should be after this same blueprint or likeness—male and female. From the study of matter, this proves to be so, everything has the atomic properties of a positively and negatively charged atom and a membrane with a nucleus that they spin around. The male progenerator, the female receives and incubates, and a uniting nucleus is the creative pattern that the material word follows.

The whole material world, visible and invisible, bares this likeness as a proof that the ancient Scripture is accurate in its account of the creation of man after the *Yetser* (Image) and *Tselem* (Likeness) of *Elohim*. If we read between the lines and paraphrase the creation story, it should say something like this . . .

After *Yahweh* was done contemplating, He expressed to the agents of creation the Elohim (wisdom, knowledge, and understanding [mental faculties and properties]) His desire and intent and formulated the pattern of force and form. Or in other words, male and female in the medium of an unseen and an undifferentiated energy substance which evolved into the various and numerous forms that He expressed and said let there be and they came into existence).

Here are the aforementioned statements in a mathematical formulation: $1 \times 1 = 1 + 1 = 2$ and $2 \times 2 = 4 \times 4^2$ to ∞. Notice that it does not start with zero because nothing from nothing leaves nothing $(0 + 0 = 0, 0 \times 0 = 0)$. He exited what we would characterize as nothing to subsist as one (beginning), and then created in an act of self-expression, leading to the dual expression of substance and form (cause and effect). Substance passed into the form of male and female (positive and negative), which diversified into the four elements: wind, fire, water, and earth. The four elements squared created a multiple and exponential duplication of itself into varieties of the self-same elements.[1]

The Creator made the epitome and a mirror reflection of all creation in the principle form of male and female. Instead of creating on the macrocosmic level He created from an individual standpoint when he made humans on Earth. He created man upon which He bestowed dominion. He gave them the stewardship over the earth as His own offspring. Here is where revolution comes into the creative process. It is at this point of creation, the sixth day as the text tells us, that a spiritual being was manifested with a soul comprising of mind, will, and emotion encased in a triple six carbon molecular structure of mass called a body. The Man made of Earth was endowed and commanded to multiply and be fruitful, replenish the earth and take dominion over it. Man inherited the substance that the Spirit brought forth from the imagination of The Self Originating Father as He willed it to be.

It should also be made clear by this that dominion over all creation on Earth is really only self-mastery because man is the summation of all that preceded him. Man is made up of all the elements found in the earth—wind (breath, *ruach* or *pneuma)*, earth (dust, subatomic particles), water (various acids and other liquids), fire (electric neurons, nerves, and an electromagnetic field), vibrations and frequencies; determining density and visibility. Man

---

1 See the Fibonacci numbers (0,1,1,2,3,5,8,13,21,34, and so forth or the "Golden Mean

has a vegetable nature needing the sun, water, and other various nutrients to live. Man has an animal nature, that gives him an instinctual drive and ambition. Man has a human nature of desire, consciousness, and will. Last but not the least, man has a G-d nature of spiritual and divine insight. To have mastery over oneself is reciprocally mastery or dominion over the earth and every living, moving thing upon it. This beginning as described in the Bible is the birth of the individual, which is designed to start the creative process of involution, evolution, and revolution over, not from the macrocosmic universal level, but from the microcosmic individual standpoint. The Ah-Dam (Man) as male and as female together was designed to create their world on earth by means of self-contemplation, imagination, verbalization, and action.

Albert Einstein, a notable scientist said: "The only true failure is to fail to imagine." Einstein understood that creation starts with consciousness and consciousness creates. To sum it up, in the image and likeness of the Father, Man was created to create and to dominate.

Ratio" brought to us by Phidas the Greek sculptor who made it known for a more advance equation of mathematics and creation.

NOTES

_____

_____

_____

_____

_____

_____

_____

_____

_____

_____

_____

_____

_____

NOTES

_____

_____

_____

_____

_____

_____

_____

_____

_____

_____

_____

_____

MANDATE II
The Existence of Man

Male and Female: An Indivisible Duality

We have already established from the biblical text that Man was Bara (created) in the *Yetser* (image) and *Tselem* (likeness) of The One omniscient mind from which all creation sprung. Let's take a closer look at the male and female dynamics as it relates to human beings existing on the earth. We will in a later mandate discuss more on duality and oneness, but here I want to make it plain that the conceptual unit named man (*Ish and Isha*), is divided into male and female, but are one whole that may appear and function as a duality. In other words, Mr. and Mrs. Ah-Dam make one species with a dual function.

Just as the positive and negative molecule spin states are different, they are joined to a nucleus making one atom with all its subatomic parts, so is Man. *As we also know that in a high spin state, the atoms become monatomic and have super conductive properties, which shows a more solid unity of energy at the back of the material. (Superconductive material repels magnetic force creating energy by pushing rather than pulling and the combined forces create a toroidal vortex of infinite power).* So, it is with the male and female dynamic of human beings and their difference of hormonal and physical constructs. Man, as male, and female are individual parts of one whole. This is where we get the term individual from; it is the combining of the words, indivisible and duality.

To divide is to half something as we are taught in math. The number ten divided by two is five, which is half of ten ($10 \div 5 = 2$). The lowest number that man can be divided into is the signature impression of its Creator (two), which is seen in the word dual. Man is indivisible beyond its duality of male and female. We can conclude this fact if nothing else that the Bible teaches that the Creator, *YHWH* is one; hence, His offspring, MAN, made in His likeness and image must be one. Even when a male and female have a baby as a result of physically joining together in the spiritual ritual of sexual relation, in which the soul gains knowledge of the soul of the other (or the other half of its self), we know that the baby is essentially the combination of the passed on DNA divided from both parents as XY chromosomes (23 and 23 equaling 46). The two become one again demonstrating the original act of the Spirit causing energy to pass into form but now from the standpoint of individualism as Man, who is an indivisible duality. The offspring from this union can be nothing other than a male or female as Man cannot be divided into anything less than it's half male or female.

At this point, we need to define the word "existence" so that we can see how man exists as male and female. The prefix ex means out, so we see this word is telling us that something is going outward.

However, existence is defined by the Webster dictionary *as the state or fact of existing; being, continuance in being or life existence shows a universal order. Something that exists; entity; being.*

We can also say that the word existence is the combination of (here is another word that is a combination of two words) exit and sustain. Existence suggests that some entity has exited from one place or state and is sustained in the state or place it moved into. Remember that we defined Spirit as an undifferentiated energy before it passes into form. I wish to call to your remembrance also that the biblical word for image means form. Existence is a product of creation at the stage of involution (self-contemplation), moving towards evolution (self-expression).

The Original Creation at the stage of involution is the mere self-contemplation of the Omniscient (all wise and all knowing) One. Once the creative process progresses to the expression of the Mind, it must exit contemplation and sustain itself in something. In the creation of man, it exited and differentiated into a complex form and pattern having a male and female dynamic. So now we have an exit of Spirit into form and the one form taking on the dynamic of an indivisible duality called male and female. If the Creator exists as Spirit, then what was He before that? And conversely, if we exist as male and female then what were we before that? It is a mystery what the Creator was and how He lives eternally other than unchanging and undivided, which is clearly evident. However, we can plainly see that Man is and always will exist as Spirit. So, the term "being spiritual" only means being ones original self.

17

We are not totally closed out from the revelation of the nature of our Creator as His name indicates something substantial about His nature. We will talk about the concept of a name in the subsequent mandates. Yet, in this mandate, it will benefit us to look at the name of *YHWH*, as it will give us some insights into the nature of the existence of our Creator.

The Egyptian name found over the arches of the temple entrance was *Nu Puk Nu* and the Hebrew equivalent *Ayer Asher Ayer* or its English rendering I Am That I Am. I Am That I Am is not just a name, but also the first person singular of the verb to be. Exodus 34:14 gives us the impression that whatever He is in essence, it is impossible for Him to change except for the apparent change of taking on a particular form or a multiplicity of forms. Change is a movement, and a movement is recorded by time. If *YHWH* is eternal and invisible; how can He change or move? Citing an example of forced movement as opposed to natural movement, the philosopher, Aristotle, said this concerning the Creator: "He is the unmoved mover, moving everything while He remains stationary in his God-ness."

The quality of motion and change belongs to time and the material plane, so it cannot be ascribed to any eternal quality of the Creator. The name I Am That I Am which we will explore later is a self-address, a statement born of self-reflection, with the purpose and effect of which is to bring to awareness and knowledge of the one doing the reflecting. *Yahweh* is perfect, His self-reflection is perfect.

Therefore, the Divine "self-reflection" of YHWH gives Him awareness or consciousness (from which creation was brought forth), and the complete knowledge that He is self-existing, omnipresent, omniscient, and omnipotent. There is only One who possess those attributes in totality, earning Him the title of The Supreme Being. We as man are not omni or self-existing as we are not the source of our own creation nor the source of the energy that sustains us. We need environment to survive and elements within that environment to live. The Creator only needs His thought and self-contemplation to exist. Man, only exists in the form and image the Creator engraved on it in the beginning stage of the creative process. Again, Man is Spirit existing in the form of a soul with a body suited for his inhabitation of the earth and other worlds that man can exist in. Man is divided into a male and female unit; This should rule out, and I hope that one day this notion will eradicate sexism and gender conflicts between the two equal sexes due to the lack of self-knowledge. To further understand the creation of man, we must look at man's triune makeup, which is another Divine reflection.

NOTES

_____

_____

_____

_____

_____

_____

_____

_____

_____

_____

_____

NOTES

_____

_____

_____

_____

_____

_____

_____

_____

_____

_____

_____

MANDATE III
The Triunity and Makeup of Man

Man is tripartite, a triune being made up of the Spirit, soul, and body, and we will break down each component individually so that we can understand how man is to optimize his power and maximize his potential to dominate and be fruitful in the worlds where he exists–as mandated by the Creator.

The apostle Paul wrote to the ecclesia, "I pray God your whole **spirit and soul and body** be preserved blameless unto the coming of our Lord Jesus Christ." (1 Thess. 5:23). Notice the order that is given: first spirit, then the soul, and then the body.

Hebrews 4:12 compares the Word of G-d to a double-edged sword, "piercing **even to the dividing of soul and spirit**, of both joints and marrow, and quick to discern the thoughts and intents of the heart."

We have discussed the Spirit already, but there is more to say of this power and the source from whom it emanates. The Spirit is called *Pneuma* by the Greeks, which is where we get the word pneumatic (something operated by air or powered by gas). It is also called *Ruach* by those who speak the Semitic languages. *Ruach* meaning breath or wind. The first properties of wind, breath, air, and so forth is movement and force. It is in motion and through its motion that we will discover its existence, or else how would we discover the wind? In Genesis 1:2 of the creation story, we see the biblical introduction of the Spirit of the Creator moving right at the outset of creation.

> *Bersheet 1:1-2 (Genesis 1:1-2) said: In the beginning YHWH bara ha shamayim vav ha eretz (created the heavens and the earth.) 2: The earth was without form, and void; and darkness was on the face of the deep. And the Spirit of YHWH was hovering over the face of the waters. 3: Then Elohim said, "Let there be light"; and there was light. 4: And Elohim saw the light that it was good; and Elohim divided the light from the darkness.*

As I was laying in the bed awoken from my usual afternoon nap, I looked out of my window and saw the leaves and small branches of a tree right outside the window moving like it was being shaken—it was shaken by the wind. However, a question came to me immediately: how do I know it's the wind, because there is nothing else visibly shaking the tree? This is the mystery of the Spirit; it is only revealed by its effect on things. It is in principle causation. It is the first causation that yields the secondary causation and the effects. If we examine the Scripture above, we can see that this is the truth that the Scripture is conveying about the Spirit's role in creation. The word *Bersheet* is a Hebrew word meaning beginning or first in sequence or perhaps, principle. Again, we defined Spirit as an undifferentiated energy before it passes into form. If you will place your focus on the words of the text, you may notice that it says the earth was without form and void and darkness was on the face of the deep. It lays out before us the condition out of which the Spirit brings something out of apparently nothing (no form [*tohu*] and void [*bahu*]) Movement is the modality of the Spirit and is the only evidence of its existence being it is invisible and beyond perception. It is the first cause of creation; before it moved, nothing could be created let alone come into manifestation. Movement is cause; therefore, it must have something to move on and the Bible describes the object on which Spirit moved as *mayim* (waters). Take note that the word *mayim* or waters is plural and here is another plural word with a singular usage that points to a unity of One rather than two or more, just like the word *Elohim*. We will return to that thought later, let us continue to uncover the mystery of the movement of Spirit.

Natural science teaches us that motion creates heat, light, and time (also known as "*The Space-Time Continuum*"). Natural science concurs with the Scripture, and it says the first thing that followed the movement of the Spirit upon the waters was sound and light (waves and particles). This concept of light must not be mistaken with the outward visible light of the sun, which did not come into play until the fourth day of creation. It is the inward light of omniscient wisdom, thought, understanding, reasoning, knowledge, illumination, vision, and imagination.

It is the beginning. And as I explained, all principle things or original creation in this instance must be involution. Involution, then evolution, followed by the repetitious and reciprocal nature of revolution; that is the creative process. Water is the medium upon which the Spirit moved in circular spiraling motion, which then becomes the uniting substance of all that is to be formed. Spirit alone intelligently determines what forms are to be manifested and how the forms will evolve and revolve. Water is the substance out of which all living things are birthed. Let us move forward to what's being said by this principle presented in the text as we examine the same universal principle working from the standpoint of individualism through man.

> *Genesis 1:6: Then Elohim said, "Let there be a horizon in the middle of the water to separate the water." 7: So Elohim made the horizon and separated the water above and below the horizon. And so it was. 8: Elohim named what was above the horizon sky. There was evening, then morning—a second day. 9: Then Elohim said, "Let the water under the sky come together in one area, and let the dry land appear." And so it was. 10: Elohim named the dry land earth. The water which came together he named sea. Elohim saw that it was good. 11: Then Elohim said, "Let the earth produce vegetation: plants bearing seeds, each according to its own type, and fruit trees bearing fruit with seeds, each according to its own type." And so it was. 12: The earth produced vegetation: plants bearing seeds, each according to its own type, and trees bearing fruit with seeds, each according to its own type. Elohim saw that they were good. 13: There was evening, then morning—a third day.*

There is something very significant about the biblical concept of water and as we see *YHWH* divided the waters above from the waters below and put an open expanse between them. There is a particular observation that can be advantaged from the Hebrew use of this division of the waters. The lower *mayim* (waters) he gathered and named seas and the upper *Mayim* was named sky or *Shamayim* (Heaven). Notice the similarity in the two words *Mayim* and *Shamayim*. The *Sha* prefix makes it skyward or heavenly waters. Remember water is the substance that Spirit moved upon as a medium of creation to manifest form. In man, the waters represent the soul of man as birthed from pure life force. The soul of man is another triune entity made up of the mind, will, and emotion—all of which is perpetually in transition and never static or concrete. Water is transitional as it is moved upon by the omniscience of the Spirit. It can produce any form of the Spirit's choosing, which is why consciousness creates. Hear the words of the spiritual teacher, *Yahshuah*, about water as He talks to a master of the Mosaic Law, Nicodemus, in John chapter 3

John 3: Yeshua replied to Nicodemus, "I can guarantee this truth: No one can see the kingdom of Elohim without being born from above." 4: Nicodemus asked him, "How can anyone be born when he's an old man? He can't go back inside his mother a second time to be born, can he?" 5: Yeshua answered Nicodemus, "I can guarantee this truth: No one can enter the kingdom of Elohim without being born of water and the Spirit. 6: Flesh and blood give birth to flesh and blood, but the Spirit gives birth to things that are spiritual. 7: Don't be surprised when I tell you that all of you must be born from above. 8: The wind blows wherever it pleases. You hear its sound, but you don't know where the wind comes from or where it's going. That's the way it is with everyone born of the Spirit." 9: Nicodemus replied, "How can that be?" 10: Yeshua told Nicodemus, "You're a well-known teacher of Israel. Can't you understand this? 11: I can guarantee this truth: We know what we're talking about, and we confirm what we've seen. Yet, you don't accept our message. 12: If you don't believe me when I tell you about things on earth, how will you believe me when I tell you about things in heaven? 13: No one has gone to heaven except the Son of Man, who came from heaven.

It should be clear from the Master's teaching that the waters above (*shamayim*) is the *kingdom of Elohim*. Inversely, the waters below must be the kingdom of man (*YHWH's* reflection on Earth.). Father *YWHW* never gave Man dominion over Heaven–He only gave Man the access to it, but dominion over the earth, which is the reason why it should be apparent. He gave man its own kingdom–man's own soul was brought forth from the Spirit to reign over the kingdom of Man. You may ask why then must a man be born again? We will cover that in detail in our mandate which talks about man's salvation, but the immediate answer is commonly known as "The Original Sin" and "The Fall of Man." I want to call your attention to the Hebrew letter M (Mem), the first and last letter in the word *Mayim*. Its very symbol is a womb and its numerical value is 40. The number forty is a redundant number in the Bible giving clue that in all its instances, it has something to do with something being birthed or having a particular beginning.

Noah was in the Ark for 40 days and 40 nights before he came out to a new beginning after the earth was destroyed by the flood. Moses was 40 when YHWH called him to deliver Israel from the bondage of Egypt. He spent 40 days on Saini's mountain in the presence of the Angel of *YHWH* and the Decalogue (The Ten Commandments) was birthed. *Yahshuah*, The Messiah, spent 40 days in the wilderness after being baptized by John, which was the birth of His earthly ministry. However, water, the number forty, the womb, birthing, and the manifesting reality is the mystery of the word *Mayim*.

The human body is said to be made up of about 70 percent water. Water is present in the cell membrane and blood plasma (power of life is in the blood). Also, man has extracellular, interstitial, and trans cellular fluids inside the organs and ocular fluids which contain water. The same holds true for the earth, it is made up of the same percentage of water mostly in the sea and in the ice caps as well as the lakes and rivers, which eventually flow back to the sea, or evaporates into the sky to be sent back down as rain.

Ezekiel 47:9: And it shall be that every living thing that moves, wherever the rivers go, will live. There will be a very great multitude of fish, because these waters go there; for they will be healed, and everything will live wherever the river goes. *There is a river that makes glad the city of our Elohim.

We hear the phrase "Mother Earth," which refers to the planet, and she is right to be titled the "Mother" because she is a subjective substance that produces various and multiuse life forms after the likeness of the seed sown into her. The womb of a woman (female) is filled with amniotic fluid (life-sustaining water). The seed of the man (male) fertilizes the egg of the woman and travels through the fallopian tubes to the fluid-filled womb, where it develops the fetus.

So, it was with creation; the energy of the Spirit met with and moved on the substance of water and planted a seed called wisdom. The spoken word (vibratory tone) brought forth the light of the world, which manifested all life on Earth as form and matter.

John1:1: In the beginning was the Word, and the Word was with Elohim, and the Word was Elohim. 2: He was in the beginning with Elohim. 3: All things were made through Him, and without Him nothing was made that was made. 4: In Him was life, and the life was the light of men. 5: And the light shines in the darkness, and the darkness did not comprehend it.

Genesis 2:4: This is the account of heaven and earth when they were created, at the time when Yahweh Elohim made earth and heaven. 5: Wild bushes and plants were not on the earth yet because Yahweh Elohim hadn't sent rain on the earth. Also, there was no one to farm the land. 6: Instead, underground water would come up from the earth and water the entire surface of the ground. 7: Then Yahweh Elohim formed the man from the dust of the earth and blew the breath of life into his nostrils. The man became a living being.

Notice in the verses above the change of words being mentioned as things transitioned from created, which is involution, to the word made, which is evolution. It is important to know that created is termed *Bara* as we've already covered–*Ex-nihlo* (something from nothing). The word made is the Hebrew word *"Asiah*. The word made *Asiah* denotes the physical, material world. Something must already be manifested before it can be made into something else. There must be at least a model or form from which to make it. So, let me ask you, were Heaven and Earth physical before this? Was Man who was made from the dust of the earth physical before this? If we follow the course of principles that involution, evolution, and revolution have carved out for us, we can answer these questions. Also understand that these Hebrew words: *Bara* (create), *Yetzirah* (form), and *Asiah* (made) hold the key to answering these questions. Nevertheless, with these Hebrew words, we will clearly see a divine progression of the Spirit, soul, and body (one essence, two forms, and a triune makeup).

What does the Scripture say of the body of Man? Yahweh Elohim formed the man from the dust of the earth and blew the breath of life into his nostrils. The man became a living being.

The dust of the earth or subatomic particles is the material substance of the body. Breath is the word *ruach* from the Hebrew word, meaning spirit, which gives an intelligent life force as well as consciousness, thus making Man a living being or a soul.

Acts 17:28: For in him we live, and move, and have our being; as certain also of your own poets have said, for we are also His children.

In Him (the Creator) we live (soul), move (Spirit), and have our being (body). Man is a triune being and we exist in all three planes of existence simultaneously. If the Spirit which was breathed into man by His Creator (life force) was to leave man, the soul of that individual is released from the body, then the body goes back to its source—the dust—from which it was formed and made. Why formed and made?

31

Formed because that is man's molecular structure and made is the result of the information inscribed upon that molecular structure as it is seen in DNA and RNA. It should be clear that the body is the vehicle made of the earth making it suitable to live in or on Earth. On the other hand, the soul is the mind, will, and emotion of the individual that governs the body. The Spirit is man's life force and life source by which he connects to *The Living Elohim* and all the spiritual world.

The tabernacle that Moses constructed in the wilderness and the sanctuary that Solomon later built after the pattern that was shown to his father, *Daud* (David), is in the likeness of man. The temple was the first *yeshiva* (school) for the Israeli priest and if one were to research, you would find that some of the more ancient temples like The Temple of Hathor (which Moses' father-in-law, Jethro, ministered as priest in) and a few other Egyptian temples were constructed the same way. They had an outer court, inner court, and an innermost secret place. The outer court is where there was natural sunlight and the altar to sacrifice for sin. *Yahshuah*, the sacrificial lamb, died outside the camp on the hill of Golgotha. The inner court which is the *Holy Place* and the *Holy of Holies* which is divided by a veil, is made to reflect the soul and the spirit of man. The inner court as the soul of man had an illuminated candlelight representing the relationship of the word of *YHWH* and the mind of man, the brass leaven or washing bowl, which represents the conscious of man that must be purged of hidden sins and secret faults. The table of showbread upon which 12 loaves of bread was placed in which 6 had to be fresh every day. It represents the heart and the will of man that must be tried, tested, confirmed, and presented to *YHWH* daily. It also had the altar of incense where a prescribed fragrance must be burned continually day and night. It also represented prayer, praise, and worship of the heart and mind of an individual dedicated to *YHWH*. It must be given in sanctification with clean hands (repentance from sin) without ceasing.

The *Holy of Holies* in the tabernacle contained the Ark of the Covenant and was the part of the temple in which *Yahweh* actually dwelt, which corresponds to the spirit of man. The spirit part of us is where *YHWH* dwells by the Holy Spirit, and where the angels or messengers of *YHWH* minister to us. (1 Corinthians 3:16; 1 Corinthians 6:19). The spirit is what we use to communicate with *YHWH*, once we are born again and regenerated by The Holy Spirit; one can consciously worship and commune with The Holy Blessed One. It also contained Aaron's rod that grew buds of flowers and almonds to prove who *YHWH* had selected as His priest.

The budding rod is a symbol of resurrection to life and a picture of the Messiah—the Rod of Jesse, the root and offspring of *Daud* (David). It also symbolizes the power of the Holy Spirit dwelling in the human spirit of man imparting divine wisdom. Our body is that with which we remain connected to the outside world. And in-between the body and spirit is our soul, where the mind, will, and emotion lay, determining whether body or spirit will have dominance (Romans 7:23; Galatians 5:17). We are to be led and guided by the Spirit who is to possess the nine offices of our mind and submerge us in pure emotions, assisting our will to dictate truth and righteousness to the body, bringing forth life unto life eternal.

NOTES

_____

_____

_____

_____

_____

_____

_____

_____

_____

_____

_____

_____

NOTES

_____

_____

_____

_____

_____

_____

_____

_____

_____

_____

_____

_____

MANDATE IV

Man's Dominion: Names and Purpose

Have you ever looked up the meaning of your name and found that it fits you? Have you ever named an animal perhaps a dog, cat, or a horse and in time its character seems to fit the name you gave it? Have you ever looked at someone or something in operation and named it based on how it or they functioned? Most of us have. Through our instincts as well as our reasoning faculties, we develop opinions about people, places, and things and then, we give them names. We can reason then that a name is how you see something; how you perceive it to be. Our name is how we perceive ourselves to be also, which has a direct impact on how we behave. A name functions just like a belief system. It's our paradigm—the lens that we view the world through, determining how we relate to it. Call a young boy a gangster enough and if he receives that mental suggestion watch and see how he begins to change his behavior to fit what he believes a gangster is. He will even start saying it of himself, "I'm a gangster." Call yourself a Muslim believing that you are, and without any divine word or miraculous sign from Allah, you will begin to associate and identify with what Muslims do.

So, what's in a name? A name, on one hand, is like our thoughts, limited to the prior knowledge we have conceived about certain things. On the other hand, names have a subconscious effect on us through race suggestion which is transferred largely through our DNA. We identify people, places, and things by names. It is a means of relating to people and the world around us. It means something to belong to a particular group, to have been raised in a particular neighborhood, to go to a particular school or church, etc. It gives us a sense of belonging and a sense of self-identity; we are instinctively tribal. It is what it means to be an individual. *Yahshuah* upon raising from the dead and ascending to the right hand of *Yahweh* was given a name above every other name identifying Him as the Master and Lord over Heaven and Earth. It is very allegorical of the evolutionary stages of Man's ascent, and how all things revolve back to its universal beginnings once it has fulfilled the purpose of The Originating Spirit from the standpoint of individuality.

Your name is not only your calling card, it also may determine how your life will unfold. Hebrew mystics have studied the hidden alphabetical and numerical energies associated with names for centuries and have found that there is a coded knowledge and spiritual power in names. The ancient alphanumerical Hebrew system (*Gematria*) can reveal what the mathematics of your name adds up to and what spiritual qualities and soul energy it attaches to you.

When you name something, you inscribe the potential to be or to do on to it. Naming something passes on an instinctive expectation that comes with the name. A large part of our identity is in our name. All throughout the ancient and biblical times, people were very careful in naming their children and even naming their dwelling places. Their belief systems were indicated in the names they chose. Often times, the prefix or the suffix of the name contained the name of the god they worshiped. Names of places and even people came on account of certain divine encounters they experienced. In the Bible, you will see that the angel Gabriel (*meaning El is my strength*) told Miryam (Mary, meaning bitterness or wished for a child) to name her immaculate born son *Yahshuah* (Salvation of *Yahuah*), for he shall "save" His people from their sins. The name *Yahshuah* means the Salvation of Yahweh.

He had a cousin named *Yochanan* (John), who was His ministry forerunner, "preparing the way of salvation." The same angel told his father *Zekharyah* (Zechariah meaning Yahweh remembers) to name his son *Yochanan* and not the customary naming after the father. If you look at the meaning of the two names, it's like many Bible names placed in the sequence have a message to tell. John or from the Hebrew *Yochanan* means *Yahweh* is gracious. From these names we see that *YHWH* remembers Man and His grace made a way for His salvation to come to man. Some names like these three were prophetic, foretelling the future or implying that this person will do something important as the name they carried gave an insight into what that important thing would be.

Destiny and fate are also associated with a name, so much so that people changed their name in an attempt to alter their fate or assist in getting them to their destiny. We can say it is superstition or just an old tradition, but we must recall that *Yahweh* changed names like Abram to Abraham and his wife's name from Sari to Sarah to fit the newly revealed destiny that was inscribed upon them by a covenant promise. *Yahweh* cut a deal with Abram saying, in effect, if you would become my servant and obey my directions, I will bless you. I will explain in more detail for those who may not know the Bible story and are unfamiliar with Hebrew letters and names. The letter H, when added to both names, is significant because H or *Hei* in Hebrew has the numerical value of five and it is symbolized by a window. *Hei* is symbolic for the wind and the breath of life, and when related to the number five, it indicates the five levels of the soul–something we will talk about in detail in a later mandate.

It is said that the eyes are the window to the soul. There are five levels to the soul of man, the fourth level is the highest that man can reach while in the flesh, while the fifth level is pure (God) nature. So, doing the math 4 + 1 = 5 or in words, Man at his wits end is graced with the power of his Creator to accomplish the impossible. If Abram, now called Abraham, was to be the father of many nations through his child by Sarai, now called Sarah, having (with a *Hei* added to her name also) this added letter now signified and solidified this promise in their minds. It became a direct reminder of the promise every time they said or heard their augmented names. On a metaphysical plane, it routed the soul towards a greater purpose and destiny which was to become the father and mother of many nations at the old age of over ninety years old.

What about Sarah's name? Her name means princess and signified the royalty of the children she was to bare for her husband. So, not only was this seed to become a great nation but a royal nation. To bring your focus to the importance of principle, it is necessary to know that Abraham the father, and Sarah the mother, are further allegories of the biblical motif of male and female made in the likeness and image of Yahweh Elohim bringing forth life and variety from an individual standpoint rather than the universal.

The word for father in Hebrew is *Abba*. Ab-rams name means exalted father, but it was altered to mean the exalted father of many. It is important to understand the fact that Abram had no children and was too old and sterile to have them—so also was his wife. Adding the letter *Hei* to their names didn't only have a mental impact on them, it allowed their will to acquiesce to the will of the Spirit who has the power to bring the dead to life or to create life in the first place (just as It had done in the beginning of creation). The promise of a child would be a sure sign that this entity asking for the sublimation of Abram was The Almighty *Elohim*.

A name has a certain ring to it if you will. It has a vibration and a frequency that may not mean anything to the conscious mind but means everything in the subconscious mind that translates those vibrations into thoughts and emotions by means of auto suggestion. The old adage, "Sticks and stones may break my bones, but words can never hurt," may be true if we were only physical. However, we are mental and emotional beings and words used in a derogatory manner hurt us very much and can damage the self-portrait of an individual as to paralyze his animal nature. Just like the roar of a lion that invokes incarcerating fear in the other animals in the wild. You don't even have to be a clinical psychologist to understand the psychological effects of name calling, just talk to a child on a playground of any school campus. Ask any couple in a relationship or sibling of a talking age.

Names may be for identification purposes; yet, they can empower or hinder one's ability to accomplish their *divinely* given assignment and destiny. How about assigning a proper name to a child or a nickname to a person? Yes, it can hinder or empower just the same even if the person does not consciously know what their name means. Looking at a lot of the names today, I don't believe folks are as careful as they should be about the name they choose for themselves and others. People name their children after their favorite movie stars or pop singer and so forth. Maybe that is how you got your name. I always ask parents who desire to do that, how much do you know about that entertainer's personal life and struggles because a name has a lot to do with the life path. Perhaps you are in the process of choosing a name for your child or animal or even your car. Ask yourself this question: What does this name mean, and would I be happy if what or whom I'm naming held the characteristics of that definition? A name is more powerful than you think.

We must go back to the book of the beginnings as the principle of first things would put forward, especially with anything dealing with Man and his Creator.

Genesis 2:19: And out of the ground the Lord God formed every beast of the field, and every fowl of the air; and brought them unto Adam to see what he would call them: and whatsoever Adam called every living creature, that was the name thereof. 20: And Adam gave names to all cattle, and to the fowl of the air, and to every beast of the field . . .

Before I progress into this teaching, I want to slide in this quick note: The word ground in this Scripture text is from the Hebrew word *Ha-Adamah* (ground or Earth). Notice the similarity of the word to the name of Adam (Adam with a *Hei* added to it, *Adamah*).

The first thing I want to illuminate from the outset is that the Scriptures say, "Yahweh brought the living creatures to Adam to *see what He would name them*." From whose perspective is this passage written? Was the Creator testing Adam or was He conditioning him for something? Since the Bible interprets itself, we don't have to look far for an answer elsewhere, it is here in the text.

Genesis 2:18: Yahweh Elohim said, "It is not good for man to be alone; I will make a fitting helper for him."

After making that statement, the narrative proceeds to our verse above and ends with the statement, *"but for the man, no fitting helper was found."* One thing which is evident is that Adam's sense of recognition was tested or built up in whatever way we view it. The man's wisdom and understanding is evident also as well as *Yahweh's* consent to whatever Adam called the creatures. Adam's first recognition was that of self; in his name you also see the name *Adamah*—the very substance of the red earth he was made from. In Hebrew, Man is the word *Ish/male or Isha/female* meaning fire and refers to the spiritual part of man. *Humas* refers to the body of man, made of Earth hence hu-man. Another interesting thing about the name Adam is that it contains the word *dam* which is the Hebrew word for blood. Just to note, a tri-unity is being displayed again at the back of the text. Blood/Dam (water) Humas/Body (earth) Ish/ Spirit (fire). It is not hard for Man to relate to the ground and everything including himself that was made from its red earth. Then there is his recognition of *Yahweh* as *Adonai* (Lord) and his own inherited ownership of all that was created on the planet.

Yet, there was no helpmate found for the man amongst all the beast of the field or the foul of the air. One may ask if Adam is filled with the wisdom of the Omniscient One then why is he looking for a helpmate amongst the animals and what has that to do with him naming them? What was going on is clear, when you understand that the wisdom of *Yahweh* does not operate in man without using the mind of man. Deductive reasoning was used as well as intuition, imagination, ascetic taste, thought, instinct, judgment, perception, and recognition.

Again, Man is made in the image and likeness of Elohim and is His reflection in the earth; Man is the son of *Yahweh*. This is not just a relationship between the Creator and the created, it is a royal father and a princely son. The son is being made to exercise his lordship by naming what he is to have dominion over. This may seem like a daunting task, to give names to everything; however, when you think about it, that is how we are wired.

We subconsciously label, name, profile, judge, etc. We name things for the sake of identifying. What makes this act of naming unique for Adam was the fact that he had no point of reference other than the Omniscient Spirit at the back of his mind causing him to intuit and discern. I always ask people to look at a certain animal and try and find a name more suitable than the name the animal was given by our father, Adam. You will discover it's very challenging for several reasons, race suggestion, and familiarity being amongst those reasons, plus the fact that this is an original act.

Later in this second chapter of Bereshit, we find that the *Adonai Elohim Yetser* (formed) a helpmate suitable for Adam and brought it to him just as he did with the other living creatures, and Adam recognized that his counterpart was the bone of his bone and the flesh of his flesh (a suitable mate physically and sexually). He saw that they had practically the same biological makeup and could reproduce children of the same form. The two have an ability to become one again as they are essentially, although they have been bifurcated in physical form. Not to get on my soapbox and preach here; however, it should be understood why sexual perversion is in opposition to the will and intent of the Self Originating Spirit. If a male was to be in sexual union with another male or an animal, Adam would have come to that conclusion. *Yahweh* would have never said it is not good for man to be alone. One is still alone, unable to reproduce or rejoin in reuniting to his counterpart in perverted acts of homosexual sex or bestiality. As the Scriptures say of it, "it is confusion." What would be the point other than sexual stimulation which one in an act of masturbation can do for the self, it does not serve its purpose.

As an insert here, I would like to address the point of the woman being made from the rib of Adam as it is written in Genesis 2;21-22

Genesis 2;21-22 And the Lord God caused a deep sleep to fall upon Adam, and he slept: and he took one of his ribs, and closed up the flesh instead thereof; 22: And the rib, which the Lord God had taken from man, made he a woman, and brought her unto the man.

WHAT IS MAN?

Why did Elohim use a rib rather than any other bone? It is a lot of popular theories and cute sayings like, "he took her from Adam's side because it was meant for them to walk side by side". Biologist find this scripture problematic because man doesn't seem to have a missing rib at all. The facts are that the rib bone is the most unique bone in the human body and what makes it so unique is that it can grow back. In case you don't know what stem cells are, in short it is an undifferentiated cell of a multicellular organism that is capable of making other cells like its self. The rib bone if surgically removed properly, can grow back and the stem cells can help other cells in different parts of the body grow and reproduce. The narrative tells us that the all wise maker of man performed the first open body surgery and applied anesthesia to Adam, took his rib and closed his side back up. He then took that rib and made woman. Bone marrow stem cell transplant and blood tissue stem cell transplantation can be used to regrow organs and other body parts. Approximately five bones in the body out of 209 bones are used to take stem cells, the cranium, vertebrae, sternum, hip and the rib bone. The safest to remove out of the five is the rib bone and it has the best regenerative stem cells. Who but the creator would know over four thousand years ago what biological scientists are just now figuring out today?

Genesis 2:23: And Adam said, This is now bone of my bones, and flesh of my flesh: she shall be called Woman because she was taken out of Man. 24: Therefore shall a man leave his father and his mother, and shall cleave unto his wife: and they shall be one flesh. 25: And they were both naked, the man and his wife, and were not ashamed.

The generic names of Man and Woman give the clue to what Adam discovered about his wife being the bone of his bone and flesh of his flesh. Even the generic names—Male and Female–speak to this same mystery. As you may already know, the words woman and female are the same as man and male just with the added prefix of wo and fe. I believe and have heard it stated that a woman is a man with a <u>wo</u>mb and <u>fe</u>male is male with a fetus. All having to do with reproduction, not mentality or makeup. So, man was given a womb and a fetus making her a receiver or in other words, form while the male remains the giver or force. We have discussed to some degree what the male (man) Adam's name means, but let's talk about the female woman's name. Adam called her *Chava* (The mother of all living).

> *Genesis 3:19: In the sweat of thy face shalt thou eat bread, till thou return unto the ground; for out of it was thou taken: for dust thou art, and unto dust shalt thou return. 20: And Adam called his wife's name Eve; because she was the mother of all living.*

Chava (Eve) is now named by her husband who sees her as far more than just the bone of his bone and the flesh of his flesh. He sees her eternal quality and divine nature. The name *Chava* has the same root as the four-letter name of G-D (Tetragrammaton) *YHVH*. The name of *Yahweh* means in general, the self-existing one and the living life giver. Adam sees his wife's divine reflection and through deductive reasoning appropriately names her the mother of all living. Here is a free nugget concerning the sacred name *YHWH*. The Hebrew and Aramaic language only have consonants with no vowels (A, E, I, O,

U). So how do they derive the name *Yahweh*? The name *YHWH* is made to *Yahweh* by adding the first letters of the names of Adam and Eve. It is said that the first *Hei* (letter H) is masculine and the second *Hei* in the name *YHWH* is feminine. So, the epitome of male and female is the mother and father of the race, Ah-dam and Chava.

We will talk more about Adam and Eve as we progress through the mandates of this book. But as it relates to names, it is imperative that I discuss them a bit more here. By the very description of the conditions that man's disobedience to the voice of *YHWH* brought, Adam again names something other than the animals; he gives the name Eve to his wife. He saw that woman reduced to her lowest was a child bearer–a giver of life. He already knew he was Adam from *Adamah* and at his lowest, he was the dust of the earth. What we have set before us in this allegory is a description of Man becoming self-conscious and discovering his triune makeup. He discovered that one part of self is divine, another part is mental, and the third part is physical.

The last two names I want to deal with are Moses and Joshua as they will become important later in another discussion.

Moses means drawn out or to draw out, and we know he was drawn out of a river after being hidden in a boat by his mother and then he later drew the children of Israel out of Egypt. Joshua or *Yoshuah* means salvation or deliverer, and we know that he delivered the Israelites in battle and brought them into the promised land that *YHWH* promised to give them as an inheritance. *Yahshuah* the Messiah (Savior; the Anointed One) of Israel and all of humanity walked in the power of both these individuals along with that of King David (whose name means Beloved), making Him a Prophet,

Priest, and King for all eternity. The Son of Man and The Son of *YHWH*, the perfect mediator, the King and mighty deliverer who drew Man out of the bondage of sin and death into the promised land of eternal life.

Luke 9:35: And there came a voice out of the cloud, saying, this is my beloved Son: hear him.

I will say here the boldest statements in this book, Genesis the first to the third chapter is the whole of the Bible and the rest is merely commenting and reiterating the same underlying principles. Also, Abraham, Moses, *Eliyahu* (Elijah; meaning *Yahweh* is The *Elohim*), and *Yahshuah* are the most important figures of the Bible as everything either emerges from them or converges to them. Abraham is like another Adam as he was the beginning of an ethnic group who would become a nation set aside to *YHWH* for the purpose of being His special messenger and priest on Earth who would know the law of life and liberty. Moses made the statement that *YHWH* would raise up a prophet like Himself, who must be heard in all things. The ones who don't hear would be cut off from the people of Yahweh. The Bible made a prophetic utterance that Elijah would come back and prepare the way for the Messiah. In the fullness of a predetermined time, a young virgin gave birth to that promised son who demonstrated His oneness with the Heavenly Father and then gave up His life as an ultimate sacrifice to bring atonement to man and his Creator.

In examining Genesis 1-3 correctly, the arguments that create sexist contention can be done away with, especially if it is over the fact that Eve was the weakest link and she was the downfall of humanity. We must remember the principle of oneness and never get so lost in the story that we forget its essence for the sake of the characters. All my life, I heard the accusations that were brought against the first woman and mother of the human family. I would ask you to look deeper than the surface and see the whole of the matter. Meanwhile, let's recap. First there is the process of Creation, Involution, Evolution, and Revolution. Then, we must consider one of the key essential teachings of the Bible and this book, Oneness. Oneness in the form of duality and multiplicity. How do we apply this formula to Man and Woman? In the story of the fall, the Bible says the woman was deceived but Adam was not deceived.

> I Timothy 2:13: *For Adam was formed first, then Havah. 14: Also, it was not Adam who was deceived, but the woman who, on being deceived, became involved in the transgression. (CJB)*

We read here that Adam was formed first, then Eve. Let's examine the creation stories of Genesis chapter one and two which gives the account of the creation of man from two different perspectives.

> Genesis 1:27: *So God created humankind in his own image; in the image of Elohim he created him: male and female he created them.*

In the above verses of Scripture, we can see both Oneness and duality being expressed. He created the one man as a male and a female. It does not give any order of who was created first or second. One must remember the difference between the Hebrew words create and form. The main difference is that create indicates the spiritual plane and form indicates the mental plane. Let's take a deeper look at chapter two and its description of *YHWH* bringing forth Man who is at this time given one name and not the separate name Male and Female. Here we see a sequence of the first and second–*YHWH* formed man and then He breathed into man the breath of life, the *Ruach*. Man's body was nothing but an earthly composition until the breath of life was given to it, then man became a living being (a soul). The living or consciously aware part of man can be nothing less than his soul (mind, will, and emotion) as the word form gives insight into what is being said.

Genesis 2:15: So the Lord God took the man [He had made] and settled him in the Garden of Eden to cultivate and keep it.

Man, who according to the first chapter was created (*bara*), not formed (*yetser*) or made (*Asiyah*), in *YWHW Elohim's* likeness and image as male and female. He is now made, according to Genesis 2:15 and placed in *Gan Edin* or the Garden of Eden (Parades, Paradise). The word Eden means well-watered. It is also called in Ezekiel the Garden of *Yahweh*. Whether this is a physical place or not is not important. One thing to note is that every good and discomforting place is experienced by the mind of man as much or more than by his body. Proof of that is: two persons can be in a tropical paradise and depending on what one perceives as pleasant or enjoyable they can be in disagreement over how they feel about the so-called paradise. As it is said, "Beauty is in the eye of the beholder." For someone, it can be perfect and for the other, it may not. For someone, the sun could be warm and comforting and for the other, that same sun can be hot and irritating. It should be evident then that the mind determines how the body feels and is what experiences a place or thing; yet, the body is the means by which that experience is initialized.

> *Genesis 2: 21b: but for Adam there was not found a helper [that was] suitable (a companion) for him. 21: So the Lord G-d caused a deep sleep to fall upon Adam; and while he slept, He took one of his ribs and closed up the flesh at that place. 22: And the rib which the Lord G-d had taken from the man He made (fashioned, formed) into a woman, and He brought her and presented her to the man. 23: Then Adam said, "This is now bone of my bones, and flesh of my flesh; she shall be called Woman because she was taken out of Man."*

The allegory takes a turn and a woman is brought out of the man and fashioned into a suitable mate and is rejoined to Adam. Just looking at the surface, this may look like a whole other creation but by following principle, we will clearly see this is in accordance with the same sequence that the earlier verse follows. It said that He formed man and then He breathed into his nostrils the breath of life. The first was purely mental involution and the second was material evolution. The breath of life, being the soul that makes Man a living creature is Eve (the mother of all living)–the woman brought out of man and brought to him for marriage. The one becomes two to become one again. The universal creation is now become reflected in creation from the individual standpoint. The One Self Originating

Spirit passes into a duel expression of substance and form to bring forth diversity and variety creating the universe.

> *Genesis 3: Now the serpent was more subtle than any beast of the field which the Lord God had made. And he said unto the woman, Yea, hath G-d said, Ye shall not eat of every tree of the garden? 2: And the woman said unto the serpent, We may eat of the fruit of the trees of the garden: 6: And when the woman saw that the tree was good for food, and that it was pleasant to the eyes, and a tree to be desired to make one wise, she took of the fruit thereof, and did eat, and gave also unto her husband with her; and he did eat.*

Some ask where was Adam when his wife was talking to the serpent? Were they not in the garden together? What end of the garden was he on when the serpent attacked Eve? It's just as much his fault for leaving his wife unprotected. Why was she so comfortable talking to a snake? Even simpler, could snakes talk or was Man able to understand animals at that time? What of the biblical statement that the woman was deceived not Adam? Why did it not affect the man when Eve ate but it did when Adam ate the fruit of the tree of the knowledge of good and evil? The man received the instructions to protect, to cultivate, to dominate, and not to eat from the tree of the knowledge of good and evil. These instructions were not given to the woman but to the man with the warning that in the day that you eat you shall surely die.

Here are the answers. Adam represents the earth and was told that from it he came and to it he shall return. Eve is called the mother of all living represented by the breath of life that made Ah-Dam a living soul. The soul or the breath of life cannot die physically, it can only be separated from its sustainer and obliviated. If it does not work or cultivate the ground it is because it didn't come from the ground. The work of the soul is mental and emotional. Adam must protect the garden from external enemies trying to invade his inner space. The woman was created to help the man not with physical strength, but mental and emotional strength, wisdom, knowledge, love, joy, peace, etc.

This allegorical principle hidden in plain sight is uncovered once we realize that a physical body (*Adamah*) cannot be deceived; yet, a soul with a mind, will, and emotions, can not only be beguiled but also make decisions and reasons. The soul is challenged by the serpent who represents the life principle in a material sense. The bible says that the serpent was more subtle than any beast of the field, this word subtle from the Hebrew is Aruwm (shrewd, crafty, sly prudent, sensible). This is a picture of the mind in reasoning with what it discovered in the outer world through the senses. The mind becomes lead astray from truth and hoodwinked. What takes place is the mind of man converts to a belief that a substance that is not the source of life can bring satisfaction. This wrong belief has converse conditions, however, and leads to lack and dissatisfaction.

Afterward, she gave the fruit (fig) to her husband and once he ate it the transgression was complete. Whatever happens in the soul eventually affects the body just as the death (cutting off) of the soul to a spiritual consciousness leads eventually to the death (cutting off from the breath of life) of the physical body. Once the body participates in what was once only a mental or emotional transgression, sin has fully conceived and produces fruit because it is experiential and no longer just conceptual. Just like thinking about adultery, murder, robbery, etc. and being deceived by its seemingly profitable reward is not a crime, once the body follows the thought with deeds then it is a punishable crime or sin.

One can see then how the woman (soul) eating of the fruit was just conceptual and mental but the man was physical, and the body (Adam) has no power to object to the will of the soul encased within it. The woman was enticed and led astray by reasoning with the senses and its outer world experience of which soul only knew in concept at this time. She saw that the tree was good for food but what she was blinded from was the fact that man shall not live by bread alone, but by every word that proceeds from the mouth of YHWH. The soul lives on mental and emotional food called wisdom and understanding not on that which could only sustain the body which must eventually go back to the dust from which it came. The Messiah said, I Am the bread of life and if a man eats my flesh and drinks my blood, he has eternal life." Eternal life is a mental/emotional state not just an indeterminate amount of time.

John 6:51: I am the living bread which came down from heaven: if any man eat of this bread, he shall live forever: and the bread that I will give is my flesh, which I will give for the life of the world 54: Whoso eateth my flesh, and drinketh my blood, hath eternal life; and I will raise him up at the last day.

This metaphoric statement rendered by Christ is speaking of real substance and the source of life as flesh and blood. The words of spirit and life that He gives, when conceived into the mental or emotional being will fructify into eternal life. With the heart man believes not with the brain or the five senses of the body. The soul of man can be saved not the body which must return to dust. However, the body being redeemed and revitalized by the Spirit has the power to resurrect some form of physical manifestation. This is made possible by believing the example that the Messiah demonstrated in His own death, burial, and resurrection. It is only by means of resurrection that the soul can enjoy eternity. After sinning, the death penalty was passed on to all souls so there is no such thing as an eternal or immortal soul without resurrection and this is why Ha Mashiach says, "I will raise him up at the Last day".

You are probably wondering what about the serpent in this narration? I have saved a whole mandate for that subject, but I will say here that the serpent in this allegory is merely the life principle of the material world. His corrupted wisdom is the inverse way of thinking and reasoning about the source of life. The belief in duality or multiple gods and also the belief in the negative as original or real substance. The power of negation is the only thing that results from the serpent's worldview of good and evil; we have clearly demonstrated that nothing from nothing leaves nothing. If one mistakenly sees duality as the starting point for creation, then the only ground to stand on is evolution proceeding to a revolution in an endless loop never reaching back to the true source of existence which is divine self-contemplation or involution.

NOTES

NOTES

MANDATE V

Man's Dominion: The Soul (A Triunity)

Now that we have discussed man as a triune being, let's take a closer look at one-third of that Triunity–the soul. Have you ever heard or wondered why people say that the number three (3) is the number of God? As you can see from the previous chapters, it is a redundant number in the divine scheme of things, and we are about to see another three-fold work of divinity in this discussion of the soul. The soul breaks down into three compartments: Mind, Will, and Emotion. And all of these have a biological counterpart through which they find manifestation. The Mind has the brain, Will has the heart, and the Emotion has the solar plexus and central nervous system. Even if most people don't know this from a scientific place, they do know it intuitively.

We say things like, "My brain gets tired from thinking too much." We sometimes confuse the brain with the mind, and we use them interchangeably. Science confirms these statements by teaching us that it is not the eyes that see nor the ears that hear but these are mental constructs created in the brain (via vibration that creates waves and particles). The brain itself sits in total darkness never seeing light nor having means to receive sound. It is the mind within that uses the brain as its connection to the outer world. We say of will, "It takes a lot of heart to accomplish tough tasks."

We speak of the will power and the heart rightfully so because they are counterparts. The relationship between emotions and the nerves (with its effect on the body) has been the subject of psychology as well as the lifeblood of the pharmaceutical industry throughout the better half of this last century. Mood enhancing drugs are made for the depressed and the hyper. The head doctor (psychologist) always relates feelings with emotional moods like anxiety. We often say things like, "I had a gut feeling about that" or "I had a feeling something was about to happen." What does it mean when one says, "You get on my nerves"? We are saying you are pricking my emotions for an emotional response. The inner emotions' connection to the nerves gives the mind a good feel for what is happening to the body. Also, the outward experience of pain or pleasure travels the nerves and plays a tune on the emotions as well.

The soul has a spirit passage that deals with the inner spirit of creativity that sits at the back of the subconscious mind. We call it the G-d nature and some belief systems call it the Holy Ghost. It also has a passage that sits behind the conscious mind which is a gate for the five senses and external environmental experience within the brain. The soul uses the brain through the mind to pass on the recorded human experiences of the thought and emotion from the first human created down to us; some term it "the collective consciousness" and as we all know, it has the ability to gather and store new experiences as well through the senses and emotions.

It should be clear from this description of the soul why *Yahshuah* the Messiah (The Perfect Soul) was both the Son of Yahweh and Son of Man. Christ is the heir of both worlds–Spirit and material–with perfect balance and precise equilibrium. He is the perfect mediator, the way or route to the higher world of G-D nature. No man can come to the father but by that Way. Christ is the arrogate of the intangible omniscient divine Spirit within, to the conscious mind of man and his outer world. *Yahshuah* said, "I can of myself do nothing," "I and my Father are one." He needed the Christ within to demonstrate the supernatural. When the power of Christ was at work in *Yahshuah* He said, "I Am the bread of life," I Am the Way, the Truth, and the Life, ". . . I Am the Resurrection and the Life." "The I Am" within man is his divine anointing and spiritual birthright.

In the art of spirituality and self-mastery, it is clear that there is no better starting place than the soul. The words of the Master in the form of a question says it best, "What does it profit a man to gain the whole world and lose his soul?" Or in other words, all physical and material gain is nothing if you lose sight of the fact that you are a soul. If that kind of importance is laid on the soul then we should be willing to learn as much as we can about the soul and as the Scripture so vehemently warns, "guard it with all diligence for out of it flows the issues of life."

The often-quoted phrases, "Money can't buy you happiness" and conversely, "Love don't pay the bills," uncovers the truth of the soul's dependence on something greater than external realities and that the material world is insufficient for the soul of man. Why do we speak of the lost soul and what is a lost soul? A lost soul is a person who may be in touch with where his or her body is physically but has no true sense of the whereabouts of his own mind, will, or emotions, nor any control over them. The greatest form of government on Earth is self-government; The Spirit of *YHWH* is the only thing YHWH designed to govern man not a written law or code of regulation. His Spirit put the heavens and Earth in order from a chaotic state at the beginning of creation and the same Spirit wants to order our lives. The Spirit gives you self-control and that is what man needs to solve all chaotic conditions. How does the Spirit help man to have self-control? It is by helping man to manage his own soul. For one to come to themselves or regain self-control, they must first bring the three components of the soul into harmony, peace, and balance with each other. One may ask how do you do that? Well, this is the lead subject of most religions, psychologists, and spiritualists worldwide.

All claim to offer means and solutions, and in part they do if it is a true practice. I don't claim to have more insight than the next on this subject, but I do know for sure that it can be achieved. I believe that the only lasting solution is that the soul must look back to its source of origination for the answer to all its instabilities. What is at the back of the soul? Where does the soul get its power from? I will attempt to answer these questions in this mandate on the soul. When trying to find the origins of anything, we must always go back to the beginning. So that's what we will do in search for the source of power and origination of the soul. The Bible explains in the book of the beginnings that the source of the soul's power is the breath of *YHWH*.

Genesis 2:7: Then Yahweh Elohim formed the man from the dust of the earth and blew the breath of life into his nostrils. The man became a living soul.

The biblical word "living soul" could also be defined as a conscious soul. The conscious soul is said to be alive versus a soul that is formed but unconscious. Entertain this observation if you would: the Scripture said, "The man became a living soul." The first chapter of Genesis deals with the creation of the "Divine Man" made in the likeness of YHWH as Male and Female (Ah-Dam). The second chapter deals with the "Soul of Man" which is only a platform of evolution to bring the Divine Man to self-consciousness or self-awareness. Know that we were Man before *Yahweh Elohim* formed us in the elements and brought our souls into being. We will be that in substance forever. The Scripture says of the Messiah that He is the same yesterday, today, and forever more. When we become self-realized, we will say the same is true of our self. Remember that the act of creation was born out of the need for divine self-expression. The soul is for the sake of the furtherance of that self-expression, but from the standpoint of the individual, as opposed to or I should say in addition to that of the universal. Before self-expression in the world of man can take place, self-awareness must be gained, and this is the purpose of the soul.

We see from the biblical text above that the consciousness of the soul that *Yahweh Elohim* formed from the dust of the ground came from the breath (*Ruach* in Hebrew) which is Spirit. We have already seen the role the Spirit played at the beginning of the creation and how it hovered over the face of the deep and activated the waters to bring forth life forms. The deep or the face of the waters find its equal in man as the subconscious mind. The Spirit moves or spirals through the subconscious mind giving inspiration (in-spiral-ation) and revelation. We say things like, "The thought came to me or the feeling rose in my heart." Where did the thought come from? Where did the feeling arise from? I merely suggest as a philosophical conjecture that thoughts and emotions arise or come from the inspiration of the Spirit moving on the subconscious mind and saying figuratively let there be light, let the waters of the subconscious mind bring forth creativity in abundance. Evidently, the Spirit is more than life force, it is an infinite intelligence. Intelligence is the quality of a mind; so then, the Spirit must be none other than one in essence with the mind of the Creator. We are back to the principle of involution transitioning from the macrocosmic universal plane to the microcosmic individual plane and progressing to evolution.

What is a lost soul? A lost soul is one that is spiritually unbalanced and cut off from the Creative Originating Spirit at the back of his own mind. All that a lost soul has to rely on is its five senses and what it has inherited from the human race suggestion (collective consciousness) passed down to it. The navigation system of a soul is the inspiring Spirit within feeding its intuition and instincts bringing a balance between inner wisdom and an outer sense perception. This is why riches could never bring joy or illicit sex can never bring lasting contentment. Separated from the source of life, the soul is being starved and a five-sense diet is like a candy bar; it gives you temporary energy but no life-sustaining nutrients. You will stay thirsty my friends. Pun intended.

The Mind of the Creator is the central processing unit that all other minds depend on for life and light. If each individual had his own mind independent of the universal mind of *Yahweh* then no two individuals would experience the world the same. Man would not have an awareness of any other person, place, or thing outside of what his own individual mind produces. What makes us aware of our environment and each other is that we are all connected to a central unifying consciousness called the Spirit. Matter is the latter stage and the lower level of the Spirit after it condescends from an undifferentiated energy substance into a manifested form. In the biblical terminology, this is the Father and the Son–which are one in essence, yet two in form–the Son of *YHWH* and the Son of Elemental Man at the same time. This is what all regenerated souls will evolve to become. Now you should see why the self-realized *Yahshuah* urged to be glorified and made one with the Father (return to His source) as He was before the world began.

> *St. John 17:5, 21, 22: And now, O Father, glorify thou me with thine own self with the glory which I had with thee before the world was. 22: And the glory which thou gavest me I have given them; that they may be one, even as we are one: 23: I in them, and thou in me, that they may be made perfect in one; and that the world may know that thou hast sent me, and hast loved them, as thou hast loved me.*

As with the universal, so it is with the individual, self-contemplation, which implies consciousness must take place as the starting point of creation. In order for man to be one with his Creator and to share in His creative power (like Man was created in the image and likeness

65

of Yahweh to do), man must have consciousness. Man is endowed with the mind power of His Creator described in the Scripture as the breath or Spirit, so we can reason that the Spirit is at the back of the subconscious mind of man and it is his source. How does the Spirit give life to the soul of man? Since the Soul is the mind, will, and emotion, then, the Spirit must feed all three aspects of the soul to keep it nourished and active. It feeds the emotions with a supply of love, judgment, beauty, joy, peace, and security, etc. Intimacy is an essential part of the makings of a healthy emotional life. It feeds the heart with feelings of hope, faith, strength, power, endurance, courage, liveliness etc. Without courage and hope, our will would be demobilized and inactively dead. I purposely saved the mind for the last because all that we are speaking of are simply mental concepts. These mental concepts or forms translate into emotional states that produce will-power. Conversely, negative thoughts produce negative emotions and being in line with cause and effect manifest negative circumstances. The Spirit feeds the mind by supplying it with wisdom, knowledge, understanding and revelation. The Spirit of the Creator gives life to the soul by taking up residence in the recesses of the mind of man to nourish its will and emotions. So, when we speak of one losing their mind or becoming emotionally bankrupt, what we are really implying is that the mind is cut off from its source which is the Spirit. The primary function of the mind is managing life as it is governed by the Spirit via the instinctive subconscious. Its secondary function is to manage the senses and emotions intuitively, along with processing all experiences.

One of the endeavors of this book is to develop and awaken the soul to its divine conscious. It is also to demonstrate the need for the balance between the intangible world of the unseen Spirit and the tangible visible world of matter. The soul of man is the medium of both worlds and is the single most important aspect of Man's existence on the earth. I however do understand that the attaining of my goal with this book is largely dependent on the stage of the development of the soul of the individual reading. No teacher could make the spiritual truth plainer and more straightforward than *Yahshuah*, yet many turned away not able to stand under His teachings. He also made it known that only His sheep hear His voice. I pray that by the mere fact that you are reading this book that your soul has evolved to the state where you can receive the teachings put forth in this body of work. The words in this book are food for your mind and the mind is absolutely the greatest commodity on the entire planet.

The mind has at least nine functions that the Spirit uses as a means to feed the soul of every man. I will list them here; however, pay no attention to the order of the listing because they all are equally important and interdependent on each other. Thought, Imagination, Aesthetic Taste, Intuition, Reasoning, Memory, Perception, Discernment, and Abstraction. The brain is a physical place in the material body of man that the mind uses to manifest these qualities and functionalities.

Look these words up and see through their definitions how they relate but are distinct in function. These functions of the mind are for the sake of the Spirit supplying the soul and body with life for a period of time needed to evolve into its Divine self-awareness and reach the highest level of atonement (a word in which is seen at-one-ment). The Bible states that "we are complete in Christ."

WHAT IS MAN?

Colossians 2: That their hearts might be comforted, being knit together in love, and unto all riches of the full assurance of understanding, to the acknowledgement of the mystery of YHWH, and of the Father, and of Christ; 3: In whom are hid all the treasures of wisdom and knowledge. 8: Beware lest any man spoil you through philosophy and vain deceit, after the tradition of men, after the rudiments of the world, and not after Christ. 9: For in him dwelleth all the fullness of the Godhead bodily. 10: And ye are complete in him, which is the head of all principality and power.

The Spirit will feed the mind with life-giving wisdom, knowledge, and understanding bringing forth health to the body and prosperity to one's circumstantial world. All that pertains to life and Divine consciousness is supplied by the Christ within, who is at the back of the subconscious mind. He will deliver this divine inheritance to the mind of man by means of the nine functions listed above. Messiah said, "The words I speak unto you are Spirit and Life."

John 6:62-64: what and if ye shall see the Son of man ascend up where he was before? 63: It is the spirit that quickeneth; the flesh profiteth nothing: the words that I speak unto you, they are spirit, and they are life.

It is for this purpose as we discussed earlier that a man must be born of the water and of the Spirit so that he can both see and enter into the kingdom of Yahweh. Now that we understand these truths it should make plain certain biblical text that relates to this subject of the soul in its evolutional rise to divine self-awareness through Christ. Here I will list a few from John the apostle's writings and one from St. Matthew.

1 John 1:1: That which was from the beginning, which we have heard, which we have seen with our eyes, which we have looked upon, and our hands have handled, of the Word of life; (For the life was manifested, and we have seen it, and bear witness, and shew unto you that eternal life which was with the Father, and was manifested unto us;)

1 John 2:14: I have written unto you, fathers, because ye have known him that is from the beginning. I have written unto you, young men, because ye are strong, and the word of God abideth in you, and ye have overcome the wicked one. 15: Love not the world, neither the things that are in the world. If any man love the world, the love of the Father is not in him. 16: For all that is in the world, the lust of the flesh, and the lust of the eyes, and the pride of life, is not of the Father, but is of the world. 17: And the world passeth away, and the lust thereof: but he that doeth the will of God abideth forever.

1 John 3:1: Behold, what manner of love the Father hath bestowed upon us, that we should be called the sons of Yahweh: therefore the world knoweth us not, because it knew him not. 2: Beloved, now are we the sons of Yahweh, and it doth not yet appear what we shall be: but we know that, when he shall appear, we shall be like him; for we shall see him as he is. 3: And every man that hath this hope in him purifieth himself, even as He is pure.

1 John 5:5: Whosoever believeth that Yahshuah is the Christ is born of God: and every one that loveth him that begat loveth him also that is begotten of him. 2: By this we know that we love the children of YHWH, when we love YHWH, and keep his commandments. 3: For this is the love of YHWH, that we keep his commandments: and his commandments are not grievous. 4: For whatsoever is born of YHWH overcometh the world: and this is the victory that overcometh the world, even our faith. 5: Who is he that overcometh the world, but he that believeth that Yahshuah is the Son of YHWH? 6: This is he that came by water and blood, even Yahshuah The Christ; not by water only, but by water and blood. And it is the Spirit that beareth witness, because the Spirit is truth. 7: For there are three that bear record in heaven, the Father, the Word, and the Holy Ghost: and these three are one. 8: And there are three that bear witness in earth, the Spirit, and the water, and the blood: and these three agree in one. 9: If we receive the witness of men, the witness of YHWH is greater: for this is the witness of YHWH which he hath testified of his Son.

Matthew 17:5: While he yet spake, behold, a bright cloud overshadowed them: and behold a voice out of the cloud, which said, this is my beloved Son, in whom I am well pleased; hear ye him.

It should be made plain from the text above that only the mind under the inspiration of the Spirit that moved on the face of the deep at the beginning of creation can know who the Son or the Father is in truth. Most understand who the Father and Son represent and what concept they hold, however, they don't understand from a working knowledge birthed from revelation or LIGHT within their own mind. You can only experience The Father and Son first hand by way of spiritual revelation. The spiritually dead hasn't been born again (spiritually rebirthed) to see or experience a kingdom higher than the kingdom of the five senses. He is only capable of operating as a man with instincts suited for his natural environment.

Now that we have dealt with the three aspects of the soul, let's take it a step further and deal with a more abstract teaching about the levels of the soul and the worlds it exists in. I will borrow the concepts and terms from Hebrew mysticism to try and convey an otherwise next to impossible teaching without this mystical interpretation. There is no need for trepidation because you may not believe in mysticism or know Hebrew. The principle of a thing does not change regardless of the outer garments of terms and vernacular it may be clothed within.

Try to see the underlying principle in all teachings regardless of what school of thought you may think holds claims to it. Knowledge and truth are the divine inheritance of all humanity. For example, a mathematician can see the principles of math in a spiritual teaching just like one studied in geometry sees shapes when he looks at something other people view as art and architecture. Each field of knowledge comes with its particular language codes and symbols. Medical doctors have a field of practice that initiates coding by using terms, abbreviations, and symbols that anyone outside of that field won't recognize immediately. One thing is certain; however, all knowledge has recognizable principles no matter how dressed up and hidden they may be under the terms and syntax. Auto mechanics speak the language of cars and all its parts. They have idioms, nicknames, and symbols particular to the field that they share commonly with all other mechanics that leave the rest of us asking, "What does that mean?" So, it is with carpenters, masons, architects, archeologist, theologians and the like. Yet, once we define the vocabulary and break the codes it becomes as plain as anything, that we were taught in grade school.

In this mandate, allow me to guide you through the field of Hebrew mysticism and define some of the languages it uses as it relates to the soul, its levels of awareness, and the corresponding worlds it was suited for.

NOTES

NOTES

_____

_____

_____

_____

_____

_____

_____

_____

_____

_____

_____

MANDATE VI

The Soul of Man and the Worlds It Exists In
The Five Levels of Soul and its Four Worlds

There are five levels of awareness that the soul can attain, and these levels of awareness have planes of existence called realms or worlds. So then, each plane of existence must correlate to the level of the soul that corresponds to it. It can be seen when using an example of the difference between how the different parts of the fish (with the gills and fins) allows it to breathe in water and a man's body (with lungs) allows him to breathe in oxygen. Physically, the body must be suited for the substance it exists in. In the case of the soul of man, a different body is not needed for each realm. The soul expresses itself or becomes conscious on these variant levels to serve the purpose of existing in multi-dimensions simultaneously. Please understand that Man exists in the four lower worlds already, yet his conscious mind is not aware of it and can only be brought to that awareness by the inspiring Spirit within him.

When *Yahshuah* asked His disciples, "Who do men say that I am?" and they gave him their consensus, Peter answered with the most correct answer: "You are the Christ the Son of the life-giving *YHWH*." Notice what *Yahshuah*'s response was, "flesh and blood (five senses and race suggestion) didn't reveal this to you but my Father in heaven . . ." (Matthew 16:13-17).

From this Scripture, we can see that revelation must come to the mind of Man to see the certain truth that cannot be ascertained by a normal state of consciousness. When the prophets of old said things like, "The hand of the Lord came upon me and I was in the Spirit," it shows that a shift in conscious awareness took place. They received divine messages or saw extra-worldly visions in the waking state like most do in a dream. In this mandate, you will see why this is possible and how it is that your mind can access other worlds, have out of body experiences, dream, remotely view, travel the astral world, have a spark of genius, and communicate with plants and animals, etc.

As I stated earlier, there are five levels of awareness that the soul can experience just like there are five senses that the body uses to bring experiences to the mind. These five levels of the soul may be described as the five ascending levels of awareness and communion (common union) with the Creator. They are called (in ascending order): 1. *Nefesh*, 2. *Ruach*, 3. *Neshama*, 4. *Chaya*, and 5. *Yechida*.

A person is born from his mother's womb with a *Nefesh* (lower soul) from the world of *Asiya*–the manifested material world. This is the physical body made of the material elements in which it exists on Earth. Without the physical body and its soul counterpart (*Nefesh*), one cannot belong to the human family. This soul plane has the greatest level of concealment of the Divine and it is the reason why some scientists (who are pure materialists) can only attribute the unseen world to phenomenum. This level of awareness relates to the left brain more than to the right hemisphere of the brain, which is the more creative and imaginative side. *Nefesh* is the lowest level of the soul's consciousness, and it is simply the awareness of the physical body and the physical world–the world of *Asiya*–the world of making and action. This awareness of the physical body is not awareness in a passive sense; on the contrary, the *Nefesh* level of soul is the life force of the body.

It is because of this connection as the life force that *Nefesh* has an awareness of the body and all physical matter. This physical awareness is a result of the enmeshing of the *Nefesh* with the physical body. As we read earlier, *Elohim* made Man's body "from the dust of the earth." He blew into Man's nostrils the breath of life (Bereishit 2:7). That breath of life is the *Nefesh* or the life force that the body received and became a living soul. The Orientals call the *Nefesh* "Chi" and have several methods for developing its energy to accomplish several supernatural things. If you notice in yoga and in various forms of meditation, one is taught how to breathe and focus on the breath to elevate the mind over the body.

This common soul level brings us to the community of the human family and all the elemental creatures in our universe above in space and below in the depth of the sea. All plants, animals, insects, and everything living has *Nefesh* or awareness at this soul level. So, to the question: Do animals have a soul? Yes, but only on this level and when the physical body expires, so does it. From the dust it came, and to the dust it shall return. This level of the soul has no real connection to the other worlds only a phantom like connection, just as the memory of a person is not the physical person only your mental image of that person. If "dogs go to Heaven" it is only because you carry them in your memory there, but they have no real existence there as higher souls do. You may find it bizarre, yet if we would lower or raise our frequencies and vibrations as to tune into every living thing that has *Nefesh*, we could easily communicate with them. We have seen individuals, called whisperers, who exercise such skill; they train animals of all sorts. There are horticulturalists that boast of extraordinary insight to botanicals and cannot only grow them but also combine their properties to make them healing herbs. Man was given dominion over everything with *Nefesh* in the world of *Asiya* and as the world of sin would have it, mentally dulled Man is largely dominated by this world rather than dominating it and all its elements. I will leave that for a subject of discussion in a later mandate. There is a world above *Asiya* and that is the world called formation, *Yitzirah* in Hebrew, and we can connect to it on the soul level of *Ruach*.

When an individual has an epiphany that awakens him to a higher realm of his soul or as it is said in my tradition is "born again," his awareness raises to the next ascending level, which is *Ruach*. The primary manifestation of *Ruach* is in the emotions. This is probably why people say: "I felt good," or "I felt an overwhelming sense of love, peace, or joy came over me when ascending into this state of awareness." Let me state this fact that every soul can and will experience this world but unless that soul is born again, they cannot live or abide here. It enraptures the emotions in the Spirit of the Creator and if one abides here he has a peace that passes understanding and a joy unspeakable and full of glory. Although the intellect may be used extensively on this level of soul, nevertheless, the primary focus of the intellect here is Divine contemplation in order to arouse the emotions. Here one may get a sense of good, a rush of optimism without any intel to serve as a point of connection. It is referred to by Hebrew mystics as "the toil of the heart," through which one comes to love *YHWH* with all one's heart. You connect emotionally to the Holy One and He becomes endeared and valuable to an individual who is conscious on this level of *Ruach*. One can experience the pure emotions of love, joy, peace, etc. Pure because it has no ego filters or any colored lens to pass through.

The *Ruach* level of soul corresponds to the world of *Yetzirah* (formation). The brain is the mind's vehicle of expression as we have seen in the previous mandate. This level of soul (*Ruach*) is also the psychic realm and relates more to the right brain than the left hemisphere of the brain, which is responsible for labeling and carrying out detailed tasks. This is the realm in which we dream, have visions, and daydream. It is recorded in the brain as different brainwave patterns: Infra-low, Delta, Theta, Alpha, Beta, Gamma). Neurologists have confirmed the shift in emotions as well as awareness when the brain moves in and out of these different wave patterns. The brainwave pattern that best correlates to this soul level is theta. Theta brain waves occur most often in sleep but are also dominant in deep meditation. Theta is our gateway to learning, memory, and intuition. In theta, our senses are withdrawn from the external world and focused on signals originating from within. It is that twilight state which we normally only experience fleetingly as we wake or drift off to sleep. In theta, we are in a dream–vivid imagery, intuition, and information beyond our normal conscious awareness. It's where we hold our subconscious stuff, good and bad, our fears, past trauma, and nightmares, etc.

WHAT IS MAN?

At the root of all our thoughts, emotions, and behaviors is the communication between neurons within our brains. Brainwaves are produced by synchronized electrical pulses from masses of neurons communicating with each other. However, backing this is the Spirit acting on the soul at this level of consciousness called *Ruach* (Spirit). This is also known in Judeo-Christianity as *the baptism of the Holy Spirit*. This baptism is not the body going down in natural water but the soul submerged in the fiery Spirit of its Creator like the waters that covered the deep before it was gathered together as a sea to let the dry land (body) appear. Remember in the creation story how the Spirit moved on the water and *Yahweh* said, "Let there be light"? This realm of the soul is only a reenactment of that cosmic event from the plane of the individual man *Yahweh* created in His likeness and image.

One may ask questions like, "Why and how do we experience things like that feeling of some invisible force pressing us to our bed paralyzing us and silencing our voices from screaming for help?" "Why do we sometimes hear voices in our head?" "Why do we see phantom like entities that are mostly invisible but somehow we see them moving as apparitions in and out of sight?" I will offer an over simplified explanation here. In fact, there is a phenomenon of being in-between two worlds or two states of consciousness. When transitioning into higher or lower worlds or experiencing the shift of brain waves, there is a transitional place where you are in-between and weird happenings take place. There was a popular television show named *The Twilight Zone* and these are somewhat twilight or in-between zones experiences that the brain has no reference for and the mind has no full grasp over.

When you dream at night in R.E.M. (Rapid Eye Movement), you are in the center of the *Ruach* level of the soul's consciousness. If you notice, it is not often that you get another world experience in this kind of dream state. Even though the dream may be strange and the movement different, you are nonetheless dreaming about people, places, and things of this world. It is said that when we sleep–conscious of dreaming or not–our soul leaves the body. I would love to ask: Where does it go? Well, metaphysically about 70 percent of the soul goes into a state of awareness of the world of *Ruach* and 30 percent stays to maintain the body in *Nefesh* as its life force according to the Hebrew mystical teachings. Daydreaming or zoning out as we say–(going out of what zone is the question).–is on the physical level of the brain. The brain moves to the alpha wave, and from this mind level it is the mind drifting from *Nefesh* to *Ruach* awareness.

When people have an O.B.E. (Out of Body Experiences), they are in that 70 percent to 30 percent soul in body ratio but in a woken state as opposed to a sleep state. It can be induced by physical trauma or emotional trauma or sometimes the Spirit induces it for the sake of spiritual experience. Astral travel happens here, also as well as remote viewing. People who master this state of awareness can travel the world from their mind going forward and backward in time–experiencing events of the so-called past, present, or future. Adept psychics access this level of the soul as well to see and make predictions and give advice to their clients. This is the world of the magicians, tricksters, skilled herbalists, energy healers, and Shaman medicine men or women. The power of this world with its innate limitations is very real and can be beneficial or harmful depending on the soul using it. One must understand, however, that this realm of knowledge gained at *Ruach* is not absolute. It is only a matter of perception that we see in parts and know in parts not in whole. Therefore, many people fall into the peril of trying to live their life dependent on this lower level of revelation, and not that which comes from a pure and absolute state of awareness. Another caution is the very real nature of malevolent spiritual forces that access these same realms and are capable of deception. The next level of the soul's awareness is closer to the absolute and yields a greater revelation of light; it is the *Neshama*.

The *Neshama* parallels the world of *Beriya* (Creation). From the teachings of *Yahshuah*, this plane is called the kingdom of Heaven. In Judeo-Christianity, this realm is also known as the infilling of the Holy Spirit. And in Buddhism, it is called the state of nirvana. The Egyptian pharaohs upon reaching this state of awareness and operating in its power became known as Sons of God and changed their name to reflect that. Most of the biblical angels that correspond to this world have the name of Elohim as a suffix for example of the same practice (this is no doubt where the ancient cultures derived this practice from). Michael (Micha-El) whose name means *like unto El*. Raphael (Rapha-El) meaning *healing El*. Uriel (El is my light), Gabriel (El is my strength), Phenuel (Face of El), etc. They hold names that show they are offspring of the One El. These are the archangels that are over the armies of the angels that suit the purpose described in their name; they are lords over that field of expertise. These archangels have been given the power of the Spirit to operate and control those realms of principalities and dominions.

Yes, we share planes of existence with the angels. This is where the concept of angels coming from Heaven comes from. The Heaven they come from is the kingdom of Heaven or the realm of creation (*Beriya*). We experience the world of creation (*Beriya*) through the level of soul called *Neshama*. The world of *Beriya* is described as one burgeoning (rapidly increasing) divine energy undifferentiated and unmanifested. It is the notion of coming into being from nothing, rather than structured or quantified existence. *Neshama* holds the concept of continuous creation (the coming into being) and sustenance of life and existence. Its awareness is not limited to things or concepts already in existence but is creative and can produce from whatever the mind imagines as it is inspired by Spirit.

You hear of divine healers throughout the ages, of men who with just a touch or sometimes a word can cause the blind to see, the deaf to hear, and the lame to walk. Individuals who are highly developed in this realm have even raised the dead back to life. This realm of awareness is not to be confused with the world below it where illusion and make believe is often the real craft being worked. This level of soul is absolute, eternal, infinite, and awesome. Visions experienced here are not partial but all-encompassing and whole. You can fully rely on the knowledge that is gained in this state of consciousness. Access to this world distinguishes the prophets from the psychics or witches. This is the plane of awareness where miracles are performed, intellect shifts to supra-intellect, pure emotions are experienced, and power is transferred from the unseen realm to the material plane in a seemingly magical but very miraculous form. It comes from the kingdom of Heaven to Earth (the kingdom of man).

Yahshuah the Messiah (man's highest known master), always revealed the source of such power. He said, "These works belong to the Father, not I" (I as in the ego or the physical or psychic man). He was in principle saying, the Creator and Self Originating Spirit that is at the back of everything is working from the kingdom of Heaven above, utilizing the soul that has gained awareness on the plane of *Neshama* in the world of *Beriya* to do its work of regeneration and reconciliation. The first temptation He encountered in the wilderness (St. John, fourth chapter) after being baptized was the temptation to turn a stone into bread and eat to prove that He was the "*Son of YHWH.*" If *Yahshuah* had done this, He would have been disconnected from the kingdom of Heaven and fallen to the kingdom below like Adam and Eve did in the Garden of Eden by relying on the world of form and magic rather than eating the Bread of Life—the soul's higher realm of *Neshama* in *Beriya*. He declared and demonstrated that man shall not live by bread alone, but by every word (*Logos*) that proceeds from the mouth of *YHWH*.

The soul level of *Neshama* (higher soul) allows the awareness to the world of *Beriya* (creation) and pierces through to the essential rather than the temporary ephemeral nature of things. The function of the *Neshama* as it relates to the mind is to gain wisdom—a concept of divine intellect—as opposed to the earthly intel, as the Bible verse states, "and the soul (*nishmat*) from the Almighty gives them understanding" (Job 32:8). As it relates to the emotional aspect of the soul, due to the profusion of spiritual light one experiences at this level, the emotions of love and peace are heightened to a much greater degree than normal. There is no effort given to stir up the emotions here. This is referred to in Hebrew mysticism as "the rapture of the heart" (*re'uta d'liba*). Here, the heart truly desires *YWHW*, and love is revealed in its fullness in the heart. This is that perfect love that casts out fear, and against such love there is no hindering or negating law. One has the concept and the feeling of loving *YHWH* "with all of your soul and all of your being." This is true shabbat, atonement and the highest Holy Day.

Things that are not physically possible are possible here. This higher dimensional plane gives Man the ability to suspend and altogether defy every lower law. There is no physical barrier to the power accessed in the world of *Beriya* (Creation). However, there are mental barriers because, remember, it is through the mind and the will aspect of the soul that the power of the kingdom of Heaven must work. It requires faith and belief to be consistent in this realm of awareness. No occasional doubt will keep you operating in this level of the soul; one must be totally convinced or sold out to the kingdom within or else his belief system in the lower and outer kingdoms will become a barrier. We see this in at least two instances in the Bible where in one case, the disciples of *Yahshuah* who had been reported doing all sorts of miracles could not cast an evil spirit out of a young man because of their unbelief. The other instance where his chief disciple, Peter, climbed out of the boat and walked on water at the command of the Master but then, the strong winds and clashing of the water changed his focus to the law of the lower kingdom and he started to sink in the water that he by the power of his connection to the soul at the level of *Neshama* was walking on. If we look at this verse of Scripture from a purely metaphysical point of view, we can see certain principles of the mind emerge. One being, whatever you focus on will increase; secondly, the winds and clashing waves of water are the memories and thoughts of the laws of the lower world that one must deny to follow Christ. To keep a strong connection and stay fruitful in the world of *Beriya*, one must be rooted in the world above it—the World of *Atzilut (Emanation)*, the perfect world or Paradise as termed in mystic teachings.

Before we ascend to the next level of soul, I would like to converse with you concerning our current state as Man. Have you ever asked yourself, "Why do we only use a small percentage of our brain?" "Why does only a small percentage of the human race have developed psychic abilities or gifts to heal, or can speak to animals and plants?" "Why is it that in the state of N.D.E. (Near Death Experiences) only certain people see the white light?" The answer in general lies in the teachings of these pages. If our brain is the vehicle of the mind and the mind is one third of the soul along with Will and Emotion, then it is logical that our mind is as untapped as our brain. Our faith in the higher level of our own soul and it is minimized by our overdevelopment and unbalanced awareness in the lower world of action and making (*Asiya*).

Though it may be factual that endorphins and chemical secretions such as DMT, dopamine, melatonin, serotonin, and the like are responsible for certain emotions being triggered and even visions being seen, it still doesn't answer the question of how the brain knows how to do what it does and how is it synced to the body in such a way. We know that the ganglions in the solar plexus act as another brain in the body regulating emotions and feelings like the brain in our heads are charged by neurons. When we get a gut feeling, a hunch, or an instinctive response to an unseen stimulant, it is the brain in our gut that makes us aware of things.

The body is designed by an intelligence to be intelligent. We are aware that the thalamus and hypothalamus along with the pituitary and pineal glands, control hormones and work in concert to alter and elevate awareness. But how? And why? This question is a problem for those who say there is not an intelligent designer of the world and also for those who contend that even if we do have a creator, he is not concerned with our day-to-day functions. I submit that there is an omniscient designer who designed the world and all that is in it. And to take it one step further, the Spirit of that designer is within its creation guiding it and performing the task necessary for it to have and sustain life. The mind, under the inspiration of the omnipresent, omnipotent, omniscient Spirit can accomplish anything it can conceive or imagine. For us to utilize more of our mind and consequently more of our brain, we must be awakened to the higher worlds that require the corresponding usage of our greater faculties. We must not quench the Spirit, but experience pure emotion, gain divine revelation, be ministered to by the angels (messengers) of light, and lose our life in this world to gain it in higher worlds.

Let us take a careful look at what *Yahshuah* said before He ascended back to the Heavenly Father.

John 14:11: Believe me that I am in the Father, and the Father in me: or else believe me for the very works' sake.12 Verily, verily, I say unto you, He that believeth on me, the works that I do shall he do also; and greater works than these shall he do; because I go unto my Father.13 And whatsoever ye shall ask in my name, that will I do, that the Father may be glorified in the Son.14 If ye shall ask anything in my name, I will do it.15 If ye love me, keep my commandments.16 And I will pray the Father, and he shall give you another Comforter, that he may abide with you forever;17 Even the Spirit of truth; whom the world cannot receive, because it sees him not, neither knows him: but you know him; for He dwells with you, and shall be in you.

WHAT IS MAN?

Messiah said in essence, the Spirit of truth is in us and with us; it is at the back of the regenerated soul assisting its evolution into its full realization as a Son of YHWH. All of creation has suffered the bondage of the lack of its full glory due to the dull consciousness of man and is waiting eagerly to be liberated.

> *Romans 8:21-24: because the creature itself also shall be delivered from the bondage of corruption into the glorious liberty of the children of G-d. For we know that the whole creation groans and travails in pain together until now. 23: And not only they, but ourselves also, which have the first fruits of the Spirit, even we ourselves groan within ourselves, waiting for the adoption, to wit, the redemption of our body. 24: For we are saved by hope: but hope that is seen is not hope: for what a man sees, why doth he yet hope for?*

The undeveloped mind of Man is stopping the evolution of the whole created world from ascending into the higher world of the kingdom of YHWH and its source of life and existence. In other words, for the world to be glorified and be experienced the way the Creator sees and knows it, Man must see and know it from that same heavenly point of view. I'm in hopes that one day we will because the scriptures maintain that there will be a new heaven and a new earth. Rev21;1

> *Isaiah 6:1-3In the year of King 'Uziyahu's death I saw Adonai sitting on a high, lofty throne! The hem of his robe filled the temple. S'rafim stood over him, each with six wings — two for covering his face, two*

for covering his feet and two for flying. They were crying out to each other, "More holy than the holiest holiness is Adonai–Tzva'ot! The whole earth is filled with his glory!" (CJB)

Isaiah the prophet had a glimpse of this pure view as He gazed heavenward and heard, "Thrice Holy is *Yahweh Eloha* of the angel armies and the whole world is filled with his glory." Imagine a place filled with the splendor of the Almighty and armies of celestial beings singing praises. It sounds like Heaven, but this prophet saw it here on the earth as he looked to Him who was seated above the circle of the earth on high yet looking low.

As the Master taught, Man must not only be born again to enter into the kingdom of Heaven, he must take up his cross and deny himself daily. Your cross o' Man is the tottering back and forth between this world below (*Asiyah*) and the ones above. The self you must deny daily is the self that has its mind and belief system rooted in the lower world trapping the soul to its confines. What you see determines what you believe, and what you believe determines what you do, and what you do determines your outcome in life. Man must realize himself and become in truth a Son of *YHWH* as he reflects the divine Holy One manifested in his own flesh and blood. The Scriptures state that they who are led by the Spirit of *YHWH* are the sons of *YHWH*.

The next level of the soul is *Chaya* (living essence), where the soul merges into a state of complete nullification of the ego and into the pure knowledge of the absolute. Here, the feeling of the individual self is lost and oneness with the vast universal is sensed. This is the place of knowing the Divine that the prophet Moses desired and

YHWH replied, "No man can see me and live." Holiness unto the Lord is the reflection that the Israelite priest saw as he gazed into the brass washing bowl located in the inner court of the holy temple. The only identity is *YHWH* and the only feeling is one with Him.

Atzitlut (Emanation) is the world that corresponds to the soul level *Chaya* and it is described as being "ONE with *YHWH* above" and "a spark of the Creator clothed within a spark of the created." This is at the right hand of the Father where Christ according to the Bible have been seated, after His earthly mission was accomplished. He is lifted up here to mediate between *YHWH* and Man. A priest after the order of Melchizedek—"King of Righteousness" (that is the order of an endless life) is who *Yahshuah* became, as he was seated far above principalities, thrones, powers, and dominions.

The soul level of *Chaya* is in essence common unity with *YHWH* as we transcend all the worlds and he condescends to meet us. In the earthly temple (which served as a pattern for the heavenly temple), this place is known as "The Most Holy Place" or "The Holies of Holies." Here, the soul's knowledge is not inductive, it is not in the immanence of Divine attributes which identifies the Spirit, differentiated and manifested in creation. But rather, with discerning what the Self Originating Spirit is not (deductive reasoning). How He is not limited or defined by the finite universe; how He is in everything, yet He is not a thing. This is the place of the High order of cherubim and seraphim who fly in His presence as He is seated on the throne saying continuously, "Holy, Holy, Holy (He is not one of us, He is not of us, He is separated and distinct from this world)." There is yet a higher level that we must leave the temple altogether to experience.

Yechida (Unique Essence)

Yechida corresponds to the level of soul called *Adam Kadmon (Primordial Man) known in Judeo-Christianity as the second man (Adam).* This second man and the last Adam is the renewed glorified man from *Yechida* that is the first in order to give birth to a spiritual race. As the first Adam was first in the earthly order giving birth to a physical race of human beings, so the second man Adam is first in the heavenly order giving birth to the resurrected Yah-Man. 1 Corinthians 15:45-49

Yahshuah, The Messiah, achieved this level of the soul upon rising from the dead and was crowned as the firstborn from the dead. If He is the firstborn, then that implies that there are others who are to follow. One purpose of The Messiah is to restore man back to His original form and essence. That essence was lost by the first Ah-Dam going contrary to the law of life. In the book of Genesis, *YHWH* gave a decree that the woman (Eve) would bring forth a Son who would defeat the seed of the serpent and overcome his power (which is sin and death).

This place, *Yechida*, is a sinless world and perfect, never having suffered a fall or any imperfection but has and always will remain complete and whole. From this plane all perfection is made possible in the lower worlds. From here, *Tikkun* (Rectify or Repair) is manifested for it is the most original world; all the other worlds are patterned from it. The soul on this plane has eternal life not just everlasting life. Eternal life is the quality of life not the quantity of everlasting life one may live. Eternity has no beginning or end; it always is and always shall be in the present tense, now. This is the world of nothingness that brought forth principle or the first things.

Yechida is before the beginning and after the ending. All emerge from it and converge back into it.

This world is not chaos as some suppose but the exact opposite. *Yechida* is perpetually the divine mental state of self-contemplation as life, love, power, peace (balance and equilibrium), beauty, and joy. This is the creative process at the highest state of involution. Just as the sublime, pure, and transcendent world of *Adam Kadmon* cleaves to and reflects the Original Infinite Light, so too does the soul at the level of *Yechida*. This is the crowned essence of the soul which is naturally and immutably bound to the Holy One. One by necessity must transcend to a state of glorification, no longer looking through a glass mirror at a dim reflection but rather face to face. The looker beholding the looker.

The Scripture says of this mental state of unity that we shall see Him as He is for we shall be like Him. This level of soul is of course the highest and purest, it is also unattainable while we exist in flesh and blood. It is inaccessible from any mental plane, for here the whole soul (Mind, Will, and Emotions) must merge and become one with the Holy Spirit. This is the full redemption of the purchased possession of the soul. Christ paid for this through His vicarious sacrificial death on the cross and secured it in His resurrection from the dead. *Adam Kadmon* is the final stage of evolution for the soul of man as the Master said, "It is enough for a disciple to be as his master but no man will be greater than his LORD." We shall be like Him for we shall experience Him as He is–I Am That I Am.

These are the levels of the soul and the worlds that correspond to them. I hope I have made it plain enough in this short and general treatment of them. This book is not designed to go into depth on this subject, as that would be a book in itself and several books have been written on this subject already. My most informative read on the subject is a book called, *Adam and The Kabbalistic Tree* by Z'ev ben Shimon Halevi. Here in this mandate, I only want to show the organization of the soul and to inform you that there are other worlds that the soul gains awareness of.

If you through scientific and spiritual means learn how to master these states of awareness, you will by nature of it be a blessing and light to men around you. You will encourage your fellow man to evolve his soul to the higher heights and deeper depths of the worlds to which his soul levels correspond. The Spirit of the Creator is the Lord and master of each world. To submit to the guidance of the Spirit is the only sure way to overcome the temptation to do evil, prosper, and do good, working no ill to others or oneself. Isaiah the prophet, after seeing a vision of the Lord, complained that he was unclean and in unclean surroundings and an angel took coals from the altar of Yahweh and cleansed his lips. Know this, the Spirit of Christ within us will purify our feelings, nature, and mind of all condemnation, resentment, guilt, regrets, or worry. He will make us be without spot, wrinkle, or blemish. He will give your soul the life-giving substance of knowledge, truth, love, joy, and peace. The eternal Spirit of Life maintains the soul and the body it has created for a given time, yet it is our responsibility to keep the soul in submission to the Spirit, and not the unclean outer world through overindulging in the senses and the temporal earthly gratification it brings.

These five levels of the soul and four worlds have innate powers and abilities to influence the outer material world as well as the inner world of mind and emotion. I wish for you readers that you may prosper and be in health, even as your soul prospers in its ascent to Divine perfection at the day of resurrection.

NOTES

_____

_____

_____

_____

_____

_____

_____

_____

_____

_____

_____

NOTES

MANDATE VII
Man's Adversary and Opposition

Who is the one standing in the way of your progress? What is opposing you so that you cannot go as high or as deep as you would like? Why is it a struggle to accomplish good things? Is there an invisible devil under the ground? And if yes, how does this underground adversary affect you daily? Is there a dragon, a serpent, or a beast of old hiding out of sight with secret powers to affect people all over the world? Some people maintain that another race of people or an alien being is the devil and is their hindrance. Some say the devil is in outer space. Some say the devil is in the sea, again, I ask if he is located in any one place how does he adversely affect the entire eight plus billion people on this planet every day? We will answer this question in general as we talk about the infamous opponent of man. As it is said, the devil is in the details. One may ask, what does this have to do with discovering what man is? Great question. To know yourself and your Creator and not know your enemy would leave you incomplete in your knowledge of self. If there is something in existence that can take your life or even hinder it, it is important for you to discover it and gain as much knowledge of it as you can.

From a physical perspective, you need to know what you are allergic to, so you won't ingest it and die. You need to know your weaknesses so you can either compensate for them or devise a defense for yourself that will protect that weak area. If this is true on the physical plane how much more on the mental, emotional, and spiritual plane? Let's see what light the book of beginnings can shed on this subject.

We have here below in Scripture what is popularly known as original sin or the fall of man. The first transgression (to go against something established, in particular a law). This fall and transgression was instigated by the serpent (Nachash phonetically naw-kh-awsh)

Genesis 3: Now the serpent was more crafty (subtle, skilled in deceit) than any living creature of the field, which the Lord G-d had made. And the serpent (Satan) said to the woman, "Can it really be that G-d has said, 'You shall not eat from any tree of the garden'?" 2: And the woman said to the serpent, "We may eat fruit from the trees of the garden, 3: except the fruit from the tree which is in the middle of the garden. G-d said, 'You shall not eat from it nor touch it, otherwise you will die. 4: But the serpent said to the woman, "You certainly will not die! 5: For G-d knows that on the day you eat from it your eyes will be opened [that is, you will have greater awareness], and you will be like G-d, knowing [the difference between] good and evil." 6: And when the woman saw that the tree was good for food, and that it was delightful to look at, and a tree to be desired in order to make one

wise and insightful, she took some of its fruit and ate it; and she also
gave some to her husband with her, and he ate. 7: Then the eyes of
the two of them were opened [that is, their awareness increased], and
they knew that they were naked; and they fastened fig leaves
together and made themselves coverings.

The narrative says, "*Ha Nachash* was more subtle (aruwm), skilled in deceit than any living creature that *YHWH Elohim* had made (*asiyah*)." First off, there are two words we can't afford to brush over if we are to apprehend the allegorical message of this text. The words "living creature" and "made." The word made speaks to something manifested and living creature speaks to something relating to the life principle of the soul (breath). As it was said of Man in Genesis 1:27: breathed into his nostrils the breath of life; Man became a living soul. The word living can mean alive through consciousness or life-giving in essence. *Yahweh* is the only one who can give the essence of life because he is the originator of it. So, we can safely assume that the serpent is an entity without the ability to give life, and just a manifested creature that enabled man to gain and expand conscious awareness. One must ask though, expanded beyond what? Truth is absolute. If you add to it or take from it, it can no longer remain truth. So, the tree of the knowledge of good and evil in the midst of the garden is the serpent's mentality and the fruit thereof is the serpent's reality (world view).

Job 12:10: In whose hand is the soul of every living thing, and the
breath of all mankind.

Job 33:4: The spirit of God hath made me, and the breath of the Almighty hath given me life.

Yahshuah said, the words that I speak to you are spirit and life (or life giving).

John 6:63: It is the spirit that quickeneth; the flesh profiteth nothing: the words that I speak unto you, they are spirit, and they are life . . . They have the power to manifest reality.

Notice how according to the Scriptures words have the power to manifest reality, and consciousness creates. Surely you have heard that, "the power of life and death is in the tongue." How is this so? What is the medium of words and manifestation? It could be nothing but the subjective consciousness (feminine principle) of Man allegorized in the Bible as the female and later called Eve (The mother of all living). As a man thinks in his heart so shall his reality be. It is logical and self-evident that false knowledge leads to a false reality and the wrong action creates adverse reactions. The Messiah quoted, "Out of the heart flows the issues of life."

The heart or the soul is the feeling or thinking part of man and the subconscious mind that rests at the back of the conscious mind. Notice in our inner speech, talking to self, we say things like, "My head is filled with thoughts." "My foot shakes on its own when I'm sleepy." "My breath seems to be short." Who is the "my" that we are referring to when talking to our self? We are admitting in a sense that we are not our body, our thoughts, or our feelings, that the real self is other than all of that. The subconscious inner being then, is the real man and is the seat of the throne of the Spirit of *YHWH* or the spirit of the devil, whoever you yield it to. Your life will be a direct result of who is on the throne dictating to the subconscious mind. We will revisit this thought shortly.

Romans 6:16 (KJV): 16 Know ye not, that to whom ye yield yourselves servants to obey, his servants ye are to whom ye obey; whether of sin unto death, or of obedience unto righteousness?

If we were to compare yourself to a computer, we would say that the monitor screen is the physical manifestation of what is on the hard drive (subconscious), and what accesses the hard drive is the memory (Ram or Rom). Random access memory (brain). Read only memory (conscious mind). Its software would be the learned behaviors and the instincts of an individual. The motherboard and keyboard are the five senses and the auto atomic system. Just like the computer, we are born with DNA (information) that determines our potential. Our environment; instincts and other factors are the execution commands that determine our actions of which the circumstances in life is displayed on the monitor screen.

Psalm 51:5: I was brought forth in [a state of] wickedness; In sin my mother conceived me [and from my beginning I, too, was sinful].

Satan is called "The Old Serpent." (Revelation 12:9). It has been supposed by many commentators that the serpent, prior to the fall, moved along erect and upright. It is quite clear that an erect mode of progression is highly incompatible with the physical structure of a serpent. Consequently, had the snakes before the fall moved in an erect mode, they must have been made entirely different than any reptile we know today or that has ever been recorded in the fossil records. The typical form of the serpent and its mode of movement were in all probability the same before the fall as after it. Serpents are said in Scripture to "eat dust," (see Genesis 3:14; Isaiah 65:25; Micah 7:17). From a natural standpoint, serpents for the most part take up their food from the ground and do consequently swallow with it large portions of dust. Yet, there is something else being alluded to in Scripture by the implication of the serpent eating the dust of the earth and being condemned to crawl upon its belly. When something is erect, it is said that it is upright. When something is prostrated, it is considered low or subjugated. Remember man and all the material world was made of the dust of the earth, so the serpent eating of it as food should be seen for what it is. He can only partake of the natural, material world and can have no diet of spiritual substance subjugating him to spiritual death and ultimate defeat. That also puts the serpent in direct opposition or enmity with the Spirit. He can only be low down (immoral) and earth-bound producing death as you can see by studying the apostle Paul's teaching on the carnal mind in the book of Romans.

Romans 8:6: For to be carnally minded is death; but to be spiritually minded is life and peace.

Throughout the east, the serpent was used as an emblem of the evil (dysfunctional and disintegrating) principle in man, the spirit of darkness (void of light or wisdom). From the nature of the mental and verbal exchange between the woman (feminine principle) and the serpent in Genesis, it does not sound like a slithering land animal at all, although the Bible calls this living creature a serpent (reptile). He is characterized as the most subtle of all the beasts of the field; a land animal has instincts, not the high intellectual faculties which this deceiving tempter here displays.

It becomes evident then that the word serpent is metaphorical, for a type of poisonous wisdom or knowledge that has the ability to create a lack of life. *YHWH* warned in the day that you eat or mentally ingest the fruit of the tree of the knowledge of good and evil you shall surely die. It will benefit the reader for me to define the Hebrew words used for good and evil. Good (*tov*) in Hebrew, Strong's #2896) and for evil (*ra*) in Hebrew, Strong's #7451. The word good is the Hebrew word *Tov*. The root of this word *Tov* is the letters *Tet-bet*, which means to prepare something to receive. We can see good as: things are as they should be, but they are also progressing toward a higher completion. They are moving toward a preordained reproduction and growth or in other words, evolution and revolution.

YHWH is at the back of the goodness that infuses creation because He is all-good. He is flourishing and dynamic, life-giving and in absolute harmony. *Tov* in short means it's beautiful, working the way it was designed to. As *YHWH* said, as He observed what He created, "It is good" and concerning man, "behold it is very good."

Evil or Ra in Hebrew is defined as broken, dysfunctional or lacking. It should be noted that the English word evil has no ancient Hebrew equivalent. While most English translations will use the word evil, it is usually the Hebrew word *ra*, which is also often translated as bad. In the ancient Hebrew, there is no such thing as an evil person or thing. To understand the word Ra from a more Hebraic understanding, this word should be understood as lack and dysfunction. G-d is both functional (as seen in the creation story of Genesis, first chapter) as well as dysfunctional (such as seen with the deluge and the destruction of Sodom and Gomorrah; lacking mercy). This good and evil are not to be mixed up with the western mindset that speaks of morality, but the balance and equilibrium of one source of power that is not anything but ever-present and available. The mistaken thought of evil as a separate power from The Almighty and a rival force to Him is the very false knowledge that creates its adverse manifestation. Just like lightning or electricity, it can be a force for life or death. But who would say it is subjectively good or evil? The serpent, then, is the symbol of the power of *YHWH*; and when used correctly, can produce life, and used conversely, can produce death. The reason why the serpent is personified as a liar and deceiver is that the principle upon which he exists is wrong thinking void of divine wisdom, producing all the dysfunction and disintegration that is in existence. The serpent is none other than the conscious mind (universally and individually) being dictated to by its external stimulants without regard to the divine guiding light of Spirit within. It is through the light of the Creator that man sees light.

The reader must keep in mind that there is only one real source of power and it is all good—evil is just the misuse of that same power. This power is known as The Spirit of *YHWH* and is not a respecter of persons nor is it prejudice. However, it is selective as implied by the many biblical inferences of the words, "the will of the Lord." It yields to those that obey, and it seeks to be used by those who are intimate with it. Deuteronomy 4:8, St. John 4:23, 24, 15:7.

What the Bible describes as blessings and cursing is the higher working of the law of cause and effect, not an arbitrary decision-making (God) with both a good and an evil nature. A blessing consequent to life; a curse consequent to death.

Deuteronomy 30:19: I call heaven and earth to record this day against you, that I have set before you life and death, blessing and cursing: therefore choose life, that both thou and thy seed may live:

So, I ask again, who is the enemy of your life? Who is your opposition? Who shall separate you from the love and life that the Creator has graciously provided for you?

When its properties and laws are followed properly, water, fire, wind, electricity or any other natural substance can give benefit for life, or it can kill you dead if its properties and laws are ignorantly mishandled or negligently used. Let us examine this truth further as we look at a few more biblical references to the serpent's dual nature of life and death, good and evil.

Psalm 58:3: The wicked are estranged from the womb: they go astray as soon as they are born, speaking lies. 4: Their poison is like the poison of a serpent: they are like the deaf adder that stoppeth her ear;

This allegory of the wicked being compared to the serpent speaking lies, having poisonous words and the deaf adder (serpent) who stops her ear, alludes to the carnal mind or nature of the flesh, which is lead astray from spiritual insight.

WHAT IS MAN?

Exodus 7:10: And Moses and Aaron went in unto Pharaoh, and they did so as the Lord had commanded: and Aaron cast down his rod before Pharaoh, and before his servants, and it became a serpent.

Moses, the Messiah of ancient *Yisrael*, was commanded by the angel of *YHWH* to take Aaron's rod, which is a symbol of power, and cast it down to the ground upon which it would turn into a serpent. Notice that upright in the hand of *Moshe* the rod (tree of life) produces miracles like opening the Red Sea and bringing water out of a rock yet being cast to the ground prostrate it turns into a serpent. So is the dual nature of Man since eating the fruit of the tree of the knowledge of good and evil. When we are upright in heart and in the hands of the Spirit of Yah, we function from a spiritual and profitable state of mind. When we are immoral (low down), we start functioning in trickery and deceit, deceiving and being deceived just as the cast down rod turned serpent.

Numbers 21:6: And the Lord sent fiery serpents among the people, and they bit the people; and many people of Israel died. 7: Therefore the people came to Moses, and said, we have sinned, for we have spoken against the Lord, and against thee; pray unto the Lord, that he take away the serpents from us. And Moses prayed for the people. 8: And the Lord said unto Moses, Make thee a fiery serpent, and set it upon a pole: and it shall come to pass, that every one that is bitten, when he looketh upon it, shall live. 9: And Moses made a serpent of brass, and put it upon a pole, and it came to pass, that if a serpent had bitten any man, when he beheld the serpent of brass, he lived.

First of all, I want to draw your attention to the similarities between the Hebrew word brass (*nechushtan*), and the brazen serpent *Nehushtant* (2 Kings 18:4). Just to drop another gleaming nugget, Cain (also called the serpent's seed) and his grandson, Tubal-Cain, were metalsmiths and artificers of brass.

Genesis 4:22: And Zillah, she also bare Tubalcain, an instructor of every artificer in brass and iron: and the sister of Tubalcain was Naamah.

As I said before, most of the biblical references to serpents are of a figurative nature, and they usually imply poisonous qualities. The wicked (Psalm 58:4), the persecutor (Psalm 140:3). This word is used symbolically of a deadly, subtle, malicious enemy which in principle is inverse thinking with ill actions leading to converse consequences (Luke 10:19)

Secondly, *Yahweh* is an *Elohim* of order and everything in creation that is manifested must have its own space and place or it becomes chaotic, destructive, and disintegrating. One law of creation is harmony through balance, and without divine harmony (peace) there could be no beauty or joy.

John 3:13: And no man hath ascended up to heaven, but he that came down from heaven, even the Son of man which is in heaven. 14: And as Moses lifted up the serpent in the wilderness, even so must the Son of man be lifted up: 15: That whosoever believeth in him should not perish, but have eternal life.

The serpent when lifted up to its rightful place as one with the principles of life becomes a symbol of health and wholeness not of deceit and death. The mind under control of the sensual man can only lead to disintegration and dysfunction mainly because it was not created to operate in that order. The mind under the influence of the Spirit within can only produce life and goodness for the whole of man, soul, and body. To this, Paul says:

> *Romans 8:11 (CJB): And if the Spirit of the One who raised Yeshua from the dead is living in you, then the One who raised the Messiah Yeshua from the dead will also give life to your mortal bodies through his Spirit living in you.*

The proper order of life is Spirit > Subconscious Mind > Conscious Mind > Five Senses.

The inverse order is Five Senses > Conscious Mind> Subconscious Mind> Spirit Mind.

The greatest enemy of Man is not an opposing devil out there somewhere, it is the lack of knowledge of the truth. Lies and false reasoning are the true poison of the serpent that concerns us as humanity. The world's problems would be solved overnight if we collectively as individuals were to know the Way, Truth, and Life that the Creator designed for us to follow. The mind needs wisdom and the right knowledge in order for Man to have dominion, to be fruitful, and to live eternally (Isaiah 5:13).

> *Hosea 4:6 (CJB): My people are destroyed for want of knowledge. Because you rejected knowledge, I will also reject you as cohen for me. Because you forgot the laws of your G-d, I also will forget your children.*

When Man loses sight of his true source of life and mistakenly perceives any manifested thing as a source of life, love, power, peace, beauty, or joy, he is committing idolatry. Just as adultery(which has the same root as idolatry) breaks the bond of oneness between a married couple, so does idolatry break the bond between man and his creative source. The breaking of the bond can only be repaired by means of an atonement. When Eve (mind and emotion) and then Adam (body and will), her husband, ate of the forbidden fruit they had no more legal rights of authority which are described as "naked." They were ashamed and covered themselves with fig leaves (material provision). *Yahweh* knew that blood must be shed to bring atonement, so He sacrificed an animal and covered them. The vicarious death of another living being transfers the innocence of the life sacrificed onto the life of the one being justified and restored back to oneness. Now that atonement had been made and man regained legal rights, he still had to be put out of the garden least he eat of the tree of life and live forever in a state of knowing good and evil, hence being able to reproduce both good and evil forever. The plan of redemption was to let man suffer death and then resurrect him with a deathless body never to die again. The tree of Life would have preserved this temporary covering of flesh and extended its decaying life form. In other words, man would have stayed in a place of lacking YHWH's glory forever if he had been permitted to eat of the tree of life.

Genesis 3:15: And I will put enmity between thee and the woman, and between thy seed and her seed; it shall bruise thy head, and thou shalt bruise his heel. 16: Unto the woman he said, I will greatly multiply thy sorrow and thy conception; in sorrow thou shalt bring forth children; and thy desire shall be to thy husband, and he shall rule over thee. 17: And unto Adam he said, Because thou hast hearkened unto the voice of thy wife, and hast eaten of the tree, of which I commanded thee, saying, Thou shalt not eat of it: cursed is the ground for thy sake; in sorrow shalt thou eat of it all the days of thy life; 18: Thorns also and thistles shall it bring forth to thee; and thou shalt eat the herb of the field; 19: In the sweat of thy face shalt thou eat bread, till thou return unto the ground; for out of it what thou taken: for dust thou art, and unto dust shalt thou return. 20: And Adam called his wife's name Eve; because she was the mother of all living. 21: Unto Adam also and to his wife did the Lord God make coats of skins, and clothed them. 22: And the Lord God said, Behold, the man is become as one of us, to know good and evil: and now, lest he put forth his hand, and take also of the tree of life, and eat, and live forever: 23: Therefore the Lord God sent him forth from the garden of Eden, to till the ground from whence he was taken.

Now that the consciousness of the serpent's mind (carnal mind) had been activated in Man, it was made known to the serpent that she would be at enmity with the woman and with each other's seed–the woman's seed would be victorious though its heel would be bruised.

All that this allegory is advising is that making the right decisions and being led by the Spirit would be a perpetual battle with the carnal mind who wants to be in charge. The carnal mind will logic without wisdom, reason without truth, presuppose rather than know, all leading to disintegration, until the seed of the Woman (The spiritual mind) is fully reborn in man, resurrecting with it the serpent mentality, and bringing it back to its divine place as one; not its fallen state as a rival force. This is what *Yahshuah* referred to in John 3:13 when He said as Moshe lifted up the serpent and in John 12:32, "If I be lifted up from the earth, I will draw all men unto me." The carnal mind and this mortal body must be lifted up through death and resurrection. The first one to accomplish that is *Yahshuah*, the Messiah, who will raise us up also.

> *John 12:30-33 (AMP): Yahshuah answered, "This voice has come for your sake, not for mine.31 Now judgment is upon this world [the sentence is being passed]. Now the ruler of this world (Satan) will be cast out. 32: And I, if and when I am lifted up from the earth [on the cross], will draw all people to Myself [Gentiles as well as Jews]." 33: He said this to indicate the kind of death by which He was to die.*

We clearly see this same metaphor being expressed in the apocalyptic book of Revelation with the woman now figured as Israel, her seed who is the Messiah and the serpent.

> *Revelation 12:1: And a great sign [warning of an ominous and frightening future event] appeared in heaven: a woman clothed with the sun, with the moon beneath her feet, and on her head a crown of twelve stars. 2 She was with child (the Messiah) and she cried out, being in labor and in pain to give birth. 3: Then another sign [of warning] was seen in heaven: behold, a great fiery red dragon (Satan) with seven heads and ten horns, and on his heads were seven royal crowns (diadems). 4: And his tail swept [across the sky] and dragged away a third of the stars of heaven and flung them to the earth. And the dragon stood in front of the woman who was about to*

give birth, so that when she gave birth he might devour her child.
5: And she gave birth to a Son, a male Child, who is destined to rule
(shepherd) all the nations with a rod of iron; and her Child was
caught up to G-d and to His throne.

Some would say that they don't believe in astrology and things like
that, but they will say when describing someone who is sick, "They
are under the weather." When misfortune comes, some say, "I guess
the stars didn't line up for me tonight." Being under the forces and
elements of this world is not the way spiritual beings govern
themselves. Our soul man is to be under the direct control of the
Spirit of the Creator. The I Am in *Yahshuah* refused to be limited to a
calendar date or a new moon or any other carnal tradition. He
declared in the face of death, I Am the Resurrection and the Life. In
the face of hunger, I Am the Bread of Life, I Am the Good Shepherd,
I Am the True Vine. I Am the Way, Truth, and the Life. Israel as a
nation was to represent all of that and they did; yet, she failed
through doubt and unbelief to defeat the serpent of opposition. The
word Israel, in essence, means pure in heart and in whose mouth is
no guile (deceit). In symbol, the Prince of Yahweh. Notice *Yahshuah's*
greeting to the brother of Peter.

John 1:47: Yahshuah saw Nathanael coming toward Him, and said
of him, "Here is an Israelite indeed [a true descendant of Jacob], in
whom there is no guile nor deceit nor duplicity!"

The ancient *Kemites* would say it like this, to those calling themselves
sons of God. "Let your words (*heku*) be truth and let the truth be your

words." The power to speak things into existence from the pureness of your subconscious mind (heart) being one with the Self Originating Spirit is the sign that you are The Son of *YHWH* as well as the son of man (Adam). This dual nature was epitomized by *Yahshuah*. He had the responsibility of destroying the works of the devil.

> *Song of Solomon 2:3: As the apple tree among the trees of the wood, so is my beloved among the sons. I sat down under his shadow with great delight, and his fruit was sweet to my taste.*

The serpent as the tempter, used food three times to lead man away from *YHWH*. The women in the garden, Israel in the wilderness, *Yahshuah* in the wilderness. We see that he attacks the intellect and the emotions to bend the will to transgress against the law of life.

With the feminine principle of man in the garden, the serpent enticed her to see that the fruit was good for food, pleasant to the eyes, and something to gain wisdom from (aside from the Spirit YHWH).

> *Genesis 3:6: And when the woman saw that the tree was good for food, and that it was delightful to look at, and a tree to be desired in order to make one wise and insightful, she took some of its fruit and ate it.*

With the Israelites in the wilderness they murmured and complained against *YHWH* and Moses because they grew tired of the manna (bread of life) that came from heaven for them.

Exodus 16: [The Lord Provides Manna] they set out from Elim, and all the congregation of Israel came to the Wilderness of Sin, which is between Elim and Sinai, on the fifteenth day of the second month after they left the land of Egypt. The whole congregation of the Israelites [grew discontented and] murmured and rebelled against Moses and Aaron in the wilderness, and the Israelites said to them, "Would that we had died by the hand of the Lord in the land of Egypt, when we sat by the pots of meat and ate bread until we were full; for you have brought us out into this wilderness to kill this entire assembly with hunger." 4: Then the Lord said to Moses, "Behold, I will cause bread to rain from heaven for you; the people shall go out and gather a day's portion every day, so that I may test them [to determine] whether or not they will walk [obediently] in My instruction (law). 5: And it shall be that on the sixth day, they shall prepare to bring in twice as much as they gather daily [so that they will not need to gather on the seventh day]." 6: So Moses and Aaron said to all Israel, "At evening you shall know that the Lord has brought you out of the land of Egypt, 7: and in the morning you will see the glory of the Lord, for He hears your murmurings against the Lord. What are we, that you murmur and rebel against us?

Numbers 21:5: So the people spoke against God and against Moses, "Why have you brought us out of Egypt to die in the wilderness? For there is no bread, nor is there any water, and we loathe this miserable food (Manna and Quail)." 6: Then the Lord sent fiery (burning) serpents among the people; and they bit the people, and many Israelites died. 7: So the people came to Moses, and said, "We have sinned, for we have spoken against the Lord and against you; pray to

the Lord, so that He will remove the serpents from us." So Moses
prayed for the people. 8: Then the Lord said to Moses, "Make a fiery
serpent [of bronze] and set it on a pole; and everyone who is bitten
will live when he looks at it." 9: So Moses made a serpent of bronze
and put it on the pole, and it happened that if a serpent had bitten
any man, when he looked to the bronze serpent, he lived.

Now with Yahshuah the Messiah being led by the Spirit, the carnal mind (or tempting serpent) wasn't so successful.

Matthew 4:1 Then Yahshuah was led by the [Holy] Spirit into the
wilderness to be tempted by the devil. 2: After He had gone without
food for forty days and forty nights, He became hungry. 3: And the
tempter came and said to Him, "If You are the Son of God, command
that these stones into bread." 4: But Yahshuah replied, "It is written
and forever remains written, 'Man shall not live by bread alone, but
by every word that comes out of the mouth of GOD.'"

It was here that the seed of the woman (true Israel) gained the victory over the lower nature of his own being and became master of his own self. Notice the sarcastic inference, "if you be the Son of YHWH . . ." *Yahshuah* was self-realized and understood that the source of life was not anything material but the very Word of the Father itself. Self-mastery was at the heart of the temptations of *Yahshuah* not a devil who had the power to oppose him. It is through the power of the Holy Spirit that we are to gain the same self-awareness and self-mastery, ultimately leading to victory over the power of disintegration (death).

WHAT IS MAN?

I asked the question earlier: who your opposition is? In short, more than any devil roaming the earth, it is man's sin nature created by the inverse and perversion of the knowledge of truth and righteousness. Misconception could never birth the right knowledge along with the right action. It could only create disharmony and transgression.

> *1 Peter 5:7-9 (AMP): casting all your cares [all your anxieties, all your worries, and all your concerns, once and for all] on Him, for He cares about you [with deepest affection, and watches over you very carefully]. 8: Be sober [well balanced and self-disciplined], be alert and cautious at all times. That enemy of yours, the devil, prowls around like a roaring lion [fiercely hungry], seeking someone to devour. 9: But resist him, be firm in your faith [against his attack—rooted, established, immovable], knowing that the same experiences of suffering are being experienced by your brothers and sisters throughout the world. [You do not suffer alone.]*

This verse of Scripture is often taken out of context and the metaphor used by Cephas is oftentimes taken literally, which removes it further from the body of the text. Let us examine this Scripture a little closer and within its context. Before we can think to deal with any outside adversary, we must first kill the cause of its existence and to do that we must go within our self.

Cephas is admonishing the believers to get their negative emotions under control by tossing them to *YHWH* who is their great caretaker. Then he is telling them to deal with their mental state which governs their actions by saying, "be well balanced and well disciplined, alert and cautious." It is here that he presents the metaphor of the adversarial enemy–being "like a lion" on the hunt for prey who is to be resisted by keeping firm to their faith and understanding that all humanity is in the same fight. I humbly submit to you that the enemy Cephas is referring to is your own carnal mind. The carnal mind will reason against the Spirit and run the imagination to the worst-case scenario, keeping you double-minded and confused. If standing firm in faith is the means of fighting the adversary, then one must conclude that he is attacking your faith through circumstances and bad feelings. I ask, what demonic power outside of you has the power to do that? It is your own carnal mind called the serpent, the adversary, or Satan. I will teach the biblically personified devil and demonic powers that are independent of our mind and will. For now, I must drive this principle home to the reader so you can be sober and fight this enemy like the Scriptures teach us to.

> *2 Corinthians 10:3-5 (AMP): For though we walk in the flesh [as mortal men], we are not carrying on our [spiritual] warfare according to the flesh and using the weapons of man. 4: The weapons of our warfare are not physical [weapons of flesh and blood]. Our weapons are divinely powerful for the destruction of fortresses. 5: We are destroying sophisticated arguments and every exalted and proud thing that sets itself up against the [true] knowledge of God, and we are taking every thought and purpose captive to the obedience of Christ.*

Again, Paul is using a war parable to point out that this battle is not happening on the manifested material plane only, but in the mind of man with its contrary to the Spirit, logic, thoughts, and self-aggrandizing ego. We must bring this mind of transgression (serpent) under the power of the Christ within, to subdue it and then lift it up as Moses lifted up the serpent in the wilderness so that whoever looked on it may live and not perish (resurrection).

So that we don't leave this mandate on the opposer, lacking substance, let me give a brief lesson on demon spirits and evil forces that are in the earth with suggestive powers and power to possess and oppress individuals.

Genesis 6:1-5: Now it happened, when men began to multiply on the face of the land, and daughters were born to them, 2: that the sons of God saw that the daughters of men were beautiful and desirable; and they took wives for themselves, whomever they choose and desired. 3: Then the Lord said, "My Spirit shall not strive and remain with man forever, because he is indeed flesh [sinful, corrupt—given over to sensual appetites]; nevertheless his days shall yet be a hundred and twenty years." 4: There were Nephilim (men of stature, notorious men) on the earth in those days—and also afterward—when the sons of God lived with the daughters of men, and they gave birth to their children. These were the mighty men who were of old, men of renown (great reputation, fame). 5: The Lord saw that the wickedness (depravity) of man was great on the earth, and that every imagination or intent of the thoughts of his heart were only evil continually.

The book of Enoch further explains that it was for this reason that *YWHW* sent a flood on the earth. Yet, he asked the Lord a question concerning the Nephilim, "What shall happen to the souls of those who will be killed in the flood?" The Lord answered back, "They will remain in the earth realm and men will worship them as demons." This is where demonologists get the phrase disembodied spirits from, but it would be just as accurate to say souls with no physical manifestation. Take a look at verse five if you will and you will see the effects of these malevolent entities. They infected the souls of men. This is still in line with the principle of the biblical teachings on the devil, that he is one with the carnal mind.

A further point is that evil spirits, whether they be fallen messengers or disembodied celestial entities, are subject to the authority of man. Once man exercises that authority by understanding that the Spirit of the Self Originating Creator is within, all must obey its word. "Casting out devils" were a common practice in *Yahshuah's* day, yet only He demonstrated that by speaking verbal commands that these illegally dwelling entities feared and obeyed.

Mark 1:27: They were all so amazed that they debated and questioned each other, saying, "What is this? A new teaching with authority He commands even the unclean spirits (demons), and they obey Him."

The Bible talks about the wars in the heavens amongst *YHWH's* angels and the serpent with his angels.

Revelation 12:7: And war broke out in heaven, Michael [the archangel] and his angels waging war with the dragon. The dragon and his angels fought, 8 but they were not strong enough and did not prevail, and there was no longer a place found for them in heaven. 9: And the great dragon was thrown down, the age-old serpent who is called the devil and Satan, he who continually deceives and seduces the entire inhabited world; he was thrown down to the earth, and his angels were thrown down with him. 10: Then I heard a loud voice in heaven, saying, "Now the salvation, and the power, and the kingdom (dominion, reign) of our GOD, and the authority of His Christ have come; for the accuser of our [believing] brothers and sisters has been thrown down [at last], he who accuses them and keeps bringing charges [of sinful behavior] against them before our God day and night. 11: And they overcame and conquered him because of the blood of the Lamb and because of the word of their testimony, for they did not love their life and renounce their faith even when faced with death. 12: Therefore rejoice, O heavens and you who dwell in them [in the presence of G-d]. Woe to the earth and the sea, because the devil has come down to you in great wrath, knowing that he has only a short time [remaining]!"

When the ultimate battle against sin and Satan is won, the Scripture is telling us in an allegorical way that we will have overcome the carnal mind and all the negative emotions that it brings. The only lasting effect of its evidence will be that which has made its manifestation in the earth realm in a percentage of individuals and on a universal level (sea). It will be a part of the race suggestion for a little space of time until the physical body is laid to rest. Those who are not born into the kingdom of Heaven and whose soul has not been regenerated by the Spirit of YHWH will be confined to a secular and carnal paradigm with no ability to repent and be saved, as is evident by the tribulation and harsh conditions that befall man and he will still shake his fist at the Creator and curse Him. The repeated reference to one-third of the text in this book is an indication of a critical mass which is needed to enact anything on a mass scale. A third is equivalent to the one part of man and creation that has no spiritual connection and that is the flesh uncontrolled by Spirit. The soul and spirit of man is the two-third that is delivered and sealed for redemption. Michael whose name means "Like unto El" is the messenger of *YHWH* that is making war with the serpent and the one-third of the messengers he drew with his tail. Isn't it interesting that Michael's name means "Like *Yah?*" The same thing that the serpent told the women: "You shall be like El knowing good and evil."

That lie is overcome through the words of testimony that we have been redeemed by the atoning blood of the lamb (Just like in Genesis 3) and brought back to the knowledge of being made in the likeness and image of the I Am. This is the pure in heart in whose mouth is no deceit, the spiritual Israel.

The enemy has but a short time on Earth when we transcend this carnal mind and rise to the spiritual heights of the kingdom of Heaven within. His wrath and wickedness will be felt and experienced by those who through the carnal senses are confined to just their lower nature of the five-sense world. Isaiah the prophet said, "Darkness shall cover the earth and gross darkness the people." The redeemed will have come to the fullness of the knowledge of Christ and will share once again the all-originating mind purifying him from the lower nature of transgression and disintegration and glorifying with a Christ nature of immortality.

WHAT IS MAN?

The salvation of the soul is simply the act of reunification with its origination. A lost soul is one that is separated from its source, its Creator. However, I'd like to remind you that I am still speaking about the universal laws as well as the supreme spiritual laws. One spiritual law state, that without the shedding of blood, there could be no removal of sin. Why is this so? Innocents are lost in transgressing the mind of the Creator and His creative force, so to regain innocence the life of the innocent must be given in exchange for the life of the guilty. In order to put an individual back in right standing with the Creator, the error must be corrected, and the penalty suspended and diverted. The essence of the Creator is life as seen in His name—I Am That I Am or *Ehyeh Asher Ehyeh* meaning the Self Existing One. When one transgresses his or her Creator, they are transgressing life and existence, and that is why death is the end result. The wages of sin is death but the gift of *Yahweh* is life and peace (harmony). The Bible teaches that the life of all flesh is in its blood.

Leviticus 17:11: For the life of the flesh is in the blood: and I have given it to you upon the altar to make an atonement for your souls: for it is the blood that maketh an atonement for the soul.

If the power of life is in the blood of a creature, and the creature is blameless and innocent, then naturally, its blood will convey that. When you go to the doctor and all your vital signs have been checked and they can't determine where or what your health issue is, they take a blood test to see further. If there is something wrong with you, it will show in your blood because it is the physical life source.

So now, to sacrifice an innocent, sinless creature and to shed its blood on behalf of the sinner is to transfer the innocence of the innocent creature to the guilty man needing atonement, erasing the debt of sin. Once the transfer has been made, just like money being transferred from one bank account to another, there is no insufficiency or lack any more which is known as a state of (*Shalom Shalum*) "perfect peace." Once righteousness has been transferred to an individual, there is no insufficiency of life, and death–it is eradicated by a lawful and legal transaction called blood sacrifice.

There is a law to everything in creation–natural laws, physical laws, universal laws, mental laws, and superseding all is spiritual laws. If you are to defy a law, you must first understand its principles and then turn it upon itself. Look at the law of displacement when it comes to making things float on water; look at the law of aerodynamics when it comes to defying gravity and making things fly; look at the mental law of attraction as it relates to creating and drawing to you something otherwise untouchable. The law of sin and death is only defied by the law of faith and righteousness. A broken law is an error that has consequences attached to it, the consequence is made known by the law of cause and effect.

Sin is the transgression of the law of life and death is its result. The kind of death the Bible speaks of is separation from the source of life which eventuates in natural physical death. All worlds are parallel, and all truth is parallel, what is true of one is true of all, as in the spirit so in the mental and natural. You can't violate a natural law without ill effects that may cause serious injury or death. To violate a law and to suspend or defy a law is altogether different. Let me state this fact, to violate it is to disharmonize with it. To defy it is not a violation but a cooperation with the law, to stay in harmony with it by using its substance in a way that benefits. The former leads to the penalty of disintegration while the latter leads to the blessing of cooperation. You must obey the law of a thing in order to use it for your benefit. Just as we have done with the laws of nature to benefit from electricity, wind, water, fire etc., so we must do with the spiritual laws. The Master said, "If you obey my commandments and the teachings that I received from the Heavenly Father, you will remain in my love and His and you can ask what you will and it will be done." Obedience is harmony and an agreement (unity) that is bound to yield power.

Deuteronomy 28:1: And it shall come to pass, if thou shalt hearken diligently unto the voice of the Lord thy God, to observe and to do all his commandments which I command thee this day, that the Lord thy God will set thee on high above all nations of the earth:

St. John 15:7: If ye abide in me, and my words abide in you, ye shall ask what ye will, and it shall be done unto you. 10: If ye keep my commandments, ye shall abide in my love; even as I have kept my Father's commandments, and abide in his love. 15: Henceforth I call you not servants; for the servant knoweth not what his lord doeth: but I have called you friends; for all things that I have heard of my Father I have made known unto you.

When *Yahshuah* told the Samaritan woman that, "*YHWH* is Spirit and those who worship Him must worship in spirit and in truth," He was in essence teaching that you must abide by spiritual laws not religious creeds to truly commune with *YHWH* and worship Him correctly. The only way to obey and abide by the spiritual laws is that one must be born again to the spiritual order that sin separated all mankind from. One must also be filled with the Spirit of *YHWH* who moves according to His will and reveals His mind and will to us. The Spirit is responsible for revealing the mind and intent of *YHWH*. The Spirit of truth is the spiritual umbilical cord connecting us to the Eternal Heavenly Father.

Just as the singular vein of the natural umbilical cord carries oxygenated, nutrient-rich blood to the fetus with two arteries that carry deoxygenated, nutrient (depleted blood) away, so Christ the intercessor and His sacrifice for sin carries our sins away, while the Holy Spirit alone transports the revelation of *YHWH* who is Spirit and seeks for receptacles of worship that He can reveal Himself to. The regenerated soul of man is enveloped in the womb of Christ suspended between the tangible physical kingdom of man and the intangible spiritual kingdom of *YHWH*.

1 Corinthians 6:17: But he that is joined unto the Lord is one spirit.

Ezekiel 36:27: And I will put my spirit within you, and cause you to walk in my statutes, and ye shall keep my judgments, and do them.

John 4:24: God is spirit [the Source of life, yet invisible to mankind], and those who worship Him must worship in spirit and truth.

Romans 6:6: Knowing this, that our old man is crucified with him, that the body of sin might be destroyed, that henceforth we should not serve sin.7 For he that is dead is freed from sin.8 Now if we have died with Christ, we believe that we will also live with him. 9 Knowing that Christ being raised from the dead dieth no more; death hath no more dominion over him.

Romans 8:26: In the same way the Spirit [comes to us and] helps us in our weakness. We do not know what prayer to offer or how to offer it as we should, but the Spirit Himself [knows our need and at the right time] intercedes on our behalf with sighs and groanings too deep for words. 27: And He who searches the heart knows what the mind of the Spirit is, because the Spirit intercedes [before God] on behalf of God's people in accordance with God's will.

The law of sin (cause) and death (effect) is at work in our carnal mind (sin nature) and is made evident by our deeds just as the law of righteousness is evidenced by the spiritual attributes that are produced in us by the abiding Spirit of *YHWH* in our mind, will, and emotions. Paul teaches about these truths in his letter to a church he was an Apostle to.

Galatians 5:17: For the sinful nature has its desire which is opposed to the Spirit, and the [desire of the] Spirit opposes the sinful nature; for these [two, the sinful nature and the Spirit] are in direct opposition to each other [continually in conflict], so that you [as believers] do not [always] do whatever [good things] you want to do. 18: But if you are guided and led by the Spirit, you are not subject to the Law. 19: Now the practices of the sinful nature are clearly evident: they are sexual immorality, impurity, sensuality (total irresponsibility, lack of self-control), 20 idolatry, sorcery, hostility, strife, jealousy, fits of anger, disputes, dissensions, factions [that promote heresies], 21: envy, drunkenness, riotous behavior, and other things like these. I warn you beforehand, just as I did previously, that those who practice such things will not inherit the kingdom of God. 22: But the fruit of the Spirit [the result of His presence within us] is love [unselfish concern for others], joy, [inner] peace, patience [not the ability to wait, but how we act there is no law.

The seed of the Woman is the spirit nature and the seed of the serpent is the sin nature and this is allegorized by *Yahshuah* the Messiah's death on the cross at the crucifixion ending in His resurrection from the dead. The law of sin and death was suspended by the law of righteousness and defied in the resurrection because *Yahshuah* had no sin and His blood testifies to His righteous life. He is the perfect sacrifice for our sins as we through faith believe that He died on our behalf and resurrected to open a way for us to have eternal life. Notice in the Scripture below how Paul uses the allegory of women to represent the freedom of Spirit vs. the law of bondage.

Galatians 3:16: Now to Abraham and his seed were the promises made. He said not, and to thy seeds, as of many; but as of one, and to thy seed, which is Christ.

Galatians 4:22: For it is written that Abraham had two sons, one by the slave woman [Hagar] and one by the free woman [Sarah]. 23: But the child of the slave woman was born according to the flesh and had an ordinary birth, while the son of the free woman was born in

*fulfillment of the promise. 24: Now these facts are about to be used
[by me] as an allegory [that is, I will illustrate by using them]: for
these women can represent two covenants: one [covenant originated]
from Mount Sinai [where the Law was given] that bears children
[destined] for slavery; she is Hagar. 25: Now Hagar is (represents)
Mount Sinai in Arabia and she corresponds to the present Jerusalem,
for she is in slavery with her children. 26: But the Jerusalem above
[that is, the way of faith, represented by Sarah] is free; she is our
mother. 27: For it is written [in the Scriptures], 31: So then,
believers, we [who are born again—reborn from above—spiritually
transformed, renewed, and set apart for His purpose] are not children
of a slave woman [the natural], but of the free woman [the
supernatural].*

Paul demonstrates perfectly in his allegory the individual under the
control of the law of sin and death which is a result of the broken
commandments and rebellion against the expressed laws of *YHWH*.
As opposed to the one under the control of the perfect law of liberty
by following the guide of the Spirit.

Sin originated because Yahweh allowed His creation to have free
will. The original sinner was not Man in the garden on Earth. The
original sinner occupied a place in the lower Heavens and was an
archangel, a cherubim, who had access to the realm of seraphim that
guarded the throne according to the book of Enoch. This angel is
described in the canonized version of the Scripture in detail, See
Isaiah 14:12-14; 1 Timothy 3:6. Other angels like Semjaza and Azazel
followed Satan's sin and rebellion and joined him in leading ranks of
rebellious angels (Revelation 12:3-9). So, there was sin in Heaven

before there was sin in the universe or on Earth. Adam and Eve's sin was largely due to being counseled by the seductive reasoning of rebellion in the guise of the serpent.

The Scripture speaks clearly to the seductive power and influence the enemy has on the earth.

1. Ruler of this world or cosmos (John 12:31)
2. Head of the kingdom of darkness (Matthew 12:26; Ephesians 2:1,2)
3. Father of rebellious people (John 8:44)
4. Father of lies (John 8:44)
5. Works in the sin nature of man (Ephesians 2:2-3)
6. Opposes the gospel (Matthew 13:19)
7. Sows weeds among the good seed (Matthew 13:39)

NOTES

NOTES

_____

_____

_____

_____

_____

_____

_____

_____

_____

_____

_____

MANDATE VIII
Christ the Redeemer: The Perfect Man

Repentance, Sin, Forgiveness, New Life in Christ some have made claim that man is God and I will not deny that, but I will ask, in what way is man God? What qualifications can one give to equal Man with the *Eloha*? No doubt, it is a secular humanist boast to say that Man is divine, yet most cannot qualify such a grand statement without bringing down the Almighty to an anthropomorphic stature. When the Messiah, *Yahshuah*, said I and The Father are one, He pointed at the supernatural and miraculous works that he had already manifested in their presence. He glorified the Father by bringing Man up and not *YHWH* down; for He produced the proof of having inherited the Father's Divine kingdom. His final act of glorifying the Father was resurrection and ascension back to the Father.

John 17:1: These words spake Yahshuah, and lifted up his eyes to heaven, and said, Father, the hour is come; glorify thy Son, that thy Son also may glorify thee: 2: As thou hast given him power over all flesh, that he should give eternal life to as many as thou hast given him. 3: And this is life eternal, that they might know thee the only true G-d, and Yahshuah The Christ, whom thou hast sent. 4: I have glorified thee on the earth: I have finished the work which thou gavest me to do. 5: And now, O Father, glorify thou me with thine own self with the glory which I had with thee before the world was. 11: And now I am no more in the world, but these are in the world, and I come to thee. Holy Father, keep through thine own name those whom thou hast given me that they may be one, as we are.

Hebrews 5:5: So also Christ glorified not himself to be made a high priest; but he that said unto him, Thou art my Son, today have I begotten thee.

Anyone boasting to be divine has not only to produce miracles or work great technology or become immortal, but rise from the dead and conquer death by the power of life. *YHWH* is life and that same eternal life must be the defining measure to decide who is one and who is equal with Him. We have discussed the four worlds and the five levels of the soul, now I will explain how the divine kingdom of YHWH and the kingdom of man at the highest world and the highest level of soul are interlaced. I will repeat here what was said in our mandate on the four worlds and the five levels of the soul of man. *Yechida* corresponds to the level of soul called *Adam Kadmon (Primordial Man) known in Judeo-Christianity as the second Adam.* This second man Adam is the renewed, glorified man from *Yechidah* that is the first in order giving birth to a spiritual race. As the first Adam was first in the earthly order giving birth to a soul (physical) race of human beings, so the second man Adam (*Yahshuah*) must be first in the heavenly order giving birth to The Yah-Man. The Scriptures follow that He who has not the Son does not have this new life abiding in him.

> 1 John 5:12: *He that hath the Son hath life; and he that hath not the Son of God hath not life.*

The resurrected and ascended One, who was and is to come, is the first to reach or go back to His divine nature in the kingdom of YHWH. Lots of men have ascended to the animal kingdom, fewer have ascended to the kingdom of man; yet, one has now ascended to the kingdom of *Yah* with the promise of many more to come. Christ is the door that every man must pass through to reach the kingdom of *Yahweh*. Either through death and resurrection or by metamorphosis, we will access the glorified body according to the apostle Paul. Read the entire 15th. chapter of 1 Corinthians before proceeding to understand this mandate better.

> 1 Corinthians 15:51: *Behold, I show you a mystery; We shall not all sleep, but we shall all be changed, 52: In a moment, in the twinkling of an eye, at the last trump: for the trumpet shall sound, and the dead shall be raised incorruptible, and we shall be changed. 53: For this corruptible must put on incorruption, and this mortal must put on immortality.*

Yahshuah said, "that for all that comes to me, I will raise him up at the last day." This is a promise that no other angel, man, or God has made. He, in essence, promised to give eternal life to all who believe in Him. There is no king, prophet, guru, grand master, potentate, no man dead or alive that has made such bold, emphatic claims. He operated in the creative power that He inherited from the Father. The same creative process that operated in the universal macrocosmic creation has found its mirror image from the individual standpoint is the microcosmic level in Christ. The true Israel and last Adam are the first born from the dead just as the earth was without form and void and darkness covered the face of the deep until the Spirit moved upon it and *Yah* said let there be light. He brought light out of darkness, something from nothing, and now he brings His Son (light of the world) out of death and darkness to ultimately bring all regenerated man to the kingdom of *YHWH* for the grand Shabbat (Sabbath Rest).

Hebrews 4:9: There remaineth therefore a rest to the people of God. 10: For he that is entered into his rest, he also hath ceased from his own works, as God did from his.

John 6:44: No man can come to me, except the Father which hath sent me draw him: and I will raise him up at the last day.

John 6: 35: And Yahshuah said unto them, I am the bread of life: he that cometh to me shall never hunger; and he that believeth on me shall never thirst 36: But I said unto you, That ye also have seen me, and believe not. 37: All that the Father giveth me shall come to me; and him that cometh to me I will in no wise cast out. 38: For I came down from heaven, not to do mine own will, but the will of him that

sent me. 39: And this is the Father's will which hath sent me, that of
all which he hath given me I should lose nothing, but should raise it
up again at the last day.

Some say life did not originate on this planet, and *Yahshuah* said
that He came down from Heaven. He is from another world and He
displayed extradimensional qualities. Some believe in time travel
and *Yahshuah*, the Messiah, said to the Yahadim of His day that
before Abraham, He was I Am That I Am. Was He a time traveler?
Some believe in shapeshifters who can change their appearance.
Yahshuah transfigured right in the presence of three of His disciples
and was seen talking with two of His ancient ancestors, Moses and
Elijah the prophet. Some believe that a highly developed master can
control the weather and the four elements. Yahshuah made the trees
wither on His command, calmed the winds, and made the sea be
still. He even caused a multitude of fish to come into the nets of
fishermen who before could not catch any fish that night. What kind
of man is He? The answer is plain: He is a Yah-Man; the same kind of
man we are to become as we develop and grow in Christ.

It is important to state that lawlessness and ignorance are the
only things that stand in the way of Man's spiritual evolution. Since
the original transgression of the law, Man has spiritually devolved
and the seed of the woman, the promised male child born as the
The-anthropos (all El-Theos and all Man-Anthro), can redeem
mankind from this disintegrating cycle. History and mythology
have proclaimed many of half-God, half-men who were powerful
and notorious in their time, none was all El and all Man. None of

them were able to give eternal everlasting life to all of humanity that is willing to receive. From Asar, Heru, Tammuz, Nimrod, Marduk, Gilgimesh, and Zues to all the subsequent heroes of all cultures, the seed of the woman was not discovered until the advent of *Yahshuah* (the embodiment of Christ) who materialized in Bethlehem of Judea. I shall speak more of Him later.

We have talked about the proverbial fall of man and original sin. We have also talked about the atonement that *YHWH* chose to redeem man by which it is the shedding of the blood of the innocent on behalf of the guilty. The first act of atonement was with an animal (lamb or sheep). The first gospel preached was the promise of salvation that *YHWH* gave the woman, "in bearing a male child you shall be saved." Of an absolute certainty, that male child couldn't have been Cain, Abel, or Seth. This Son would be for a future time to come, but the story of their lives do bare some striking revelation to the need of the Messiah. Yes indeed, back to Genesis, as I already stated, everything else in the Bible is just further commentary telling the same truth in principle as the first few chapters of Genesis.

Genesis 4 (AMP): Now the man [a]Adam knew Eve as his wife, and she conceived and gave birth to Cain, and she said, "I have obtained a man (baby boy, son) with the help of YHWH." 2: And [later] she gave birth to his brother Abel. Now Abel kept the flocks [of sheep and goats], but Cain cultivated the ground. 3: And in the course of time Cain brought to the YHWH an offering of the fruit of the ground. 4: But Abel brought [an offering of] the [finest] firstborn of his flock and the [b]fat portions. And the Lord had respect (regard) for Abel and for his offering; 5: but for Cain and his offering He had no respect. So Cain became extremely angry (indignant), and [c]he looked annoyed and hostile. 6: And the Lord said to Cain, "Why are you so angry? And why do you look annoyed? 7 If you do well [believing Me and doing what is acceptable and pleasing to Me], will you not be accepted? And if you do not do well [but ignore My instruction], sin crouches at your door; its desire is for you [to overpower you], but you must master it." 8: Cain talked with Abel his brother [about what God had said]. And when they were [alone, working] in the field, Cain [d]attacked Abel his brother and killed him. 9: Then YHWH said to Cain, "Where is Abel your brother?" And he [lied and] said, "I do not know. Am I my brother's keeper?" 10: YHWH said, "What have you done? The voice of your brother's [innocent] blood is crying out to Me from the ground [for justice]. 11: And now you are cursed from the ground, which has opened its mouth to receive your brother's [shed] blood from your hand. 12: When you cultivate the ground, it shall no longer yield its strength [it will resist producing good crops] for you; you shall be a fugitive and a vagabond [roaming aimlessly] on the earth [in perpetual exile without a home, a degraded outcast].

If Cain is the serpent's seed (mental offspring), then you can see right away why he thinks differently from Abel and why his idea of worship was disobedience. Most are not aware of what this sacrificial offering to *YHWH* is all about. This ritual is what is now known as the Day of Atonement or *Yom Kippur* to the Israelites (Leviticus 23:27-28). Cain is very wise in the carnal sense and his reasoning is based on his outer stimulation through the five senses rather than his higher intuitive nature of being led by the Spirit. (Hence, a cultivator of the ground.) Keep this biblical narrative and its symbolism in line with the principles described in the mandates above and you will have the proper measurements to lay the stones of your metaphysical pyramid straight.

Notice again the body, Cain (*Qayin*), came first then the breath of life, Abel (*Havel*).

The Hebrew definition of Cain (*qayinis*), is spear or smith (weapon), and it is where we get the word metalsmith from. Watch the good and evil concept (as with the forbidden tree in the midst of the garden) that plays evenly into this name. A maker of tools (good) and a maker of weapons (evil). Tools, however, can be used to make something evil and a weapon can be used to defend one's self–good and evil depending on the mindset and the intent of the one using it. The Hebrew meaning of *Hebhel* (Abel) is breath and vapor. *Hebhel* represents the intuitive aspect of the living, conscious man that is inclined toward *YHWH* as opposed to the flesh and carnal mind that is at enmity with *YHWH*. He symbolizes the spark of divinity that is in every living, breathing creature. In the Psalms it says, "let everything that has breath (Hevhel) praise *YHWH*." Cain and Abel symbolize also the works of the analytical mind versus the subjective mind. The former is pure reasoning while the latter is reciprocal and integrating. With this in mind, let us take another look at the Scriptures and see how they function and relate.

Genesis 4:3: And in the course of time Cain brought to YHWH an offering of the fruit of the ground. 4: But Abel brought [an offering of] the [finest] firstborn of his flock and the [b]fat portions. And YHWH had respect (regard) for Abel and his offering; 5: but for Cain and his offering He had no respect. So Cain became extremely angry (indignant), and [c]he looked annoyed and hostile.

First of all, we know that the works of the flesh (fruit of the ground or the result of carnal reasoning) could never bring atonement with *YHWH*. Secondly, it is not what *YHWH* requires, so why would or should *Yah* respect it at all? Reasoning without emotions leads to cold un-regarding discernment as opposed to heartfelt reciprocal thought and intuition. *Qayin's* anger and attitude shows the outward part of his disregard. There is no repentance in him nor is it about him getting it right or gaining atonement. It's clearly about him getting his way because his form of reasoning has no emotion of love, which amounts to rebellion. The impulsive, entitled, and self-serving nature of the carnal mind is clearly seen here.

The first bold-faced lie was told, and the first murder was committed, but this was no ordinary homicide. *Qayin* in a very matter of fact way gave *YHWH* a real sacrifice by "slaying" his brother on the Day of Atonement, as to say the blood of an animal cannot truly atone for a human; a man must die for a man. Though in transgression and ill willed, it is in fact true. So, he deduced rightly but with the wrong mindset. *YHWH* had already made provision for that sacrifice to be given (The Messiah), yet in His own time and own way. For starters, Abel was just not that man who could provide a sinless sacrifice of atonement, even though his spirit was to foreshadow that a man born of the woman to die for the sins of the world. This would be the means of ultimate atonement. Abel's blood cried out from the ground for justice against his brother. Our soul cries out to *YHWH* every time our sin nature gets us in enough trouble and creates negative emotions such as sorrow, depression, anxiety, etc. I wish to implement some philosophical truth here about Cain's blood sacrifice of his despised brother. In the text it states that YHWH cursed Qayin from the earth because Abel's blood was crying out from the ground. This is the first mention of man being cursed from the earth. Let's examine this deeper. Abel's blood cried out to YHWH and He curses Cain from the ground that drank Abel's blood. Keeping in mind that this was a ritual murder, Cain sacrificed on the earth which is YHWH's altar. Yes, the whole earth is YHWH's altar and as human history evolves you will see how idolaters sacrificed to other gods causing YHWH to be angry. Even Israel took on the custom of sacrificing to false gods bringing the wrath of YHWH upon themselves. Noah later, after the flood waters dissipated, built an altar and sacrificed to YHWH and in response YHWH was so pleased that He promised He would no longer curse the earth and provided the rainbow as a reminder.

Genesis 8:20-22: And Noah built an altar unto the Lord; and took every clean beast, and of every clean fowl, and offered burnt offerings on the altar. 21: And the Lord smelled a sweet savour; and the Lord said in his heart, I will not again curse the ground any more for man's sake; for the imagination of man's heart is evil from his youth; neither will I again smite any more everything living, as I have done. 22: While the earth remaineth, seedtime and harvest, and cold and heat, and summer and winter, and day and night shall not cease.

Back to the heart of the subject, the repentant soul recognizes its need for spiritual reconnection and renewal. The carnal man will only make rationalizations and justifications for his sin and will arrogantly point the finger at others including the Creator. We see no repentance, no real remorse, only suppressed guilt and sorrow over ill consequences that the law of cause and effect brings full circle back to any individual who commits transgressions. Most times, when man reaps what he has sown, the carnal mind will not make the connection that his negative circumstances are his own doing but will declare the unfairness of it all and take on a victim mentality.

This is what *Qayin* did upon the announcement of the effects of what he did (the curse) when it was declared by *YHWH* to him. Even when man becomes sorrowful for the consequences of his deeds, it still will not lead him to repent (turn from not to turn to again) largely because of the mind's ability to justify and rationalize. Repentance is not a carnal quality, but rather a spiritual one, which then requires a move of Spirit to take place. Repentance involves an act of mercy where the superior being stoops down to the inferior being and brings them to a meeting place to reason together. It takes a soul that is sensitive to the Spirit of *YHWH* and receptive to its conviction to get beyond the carnal reasoning and to the higher reasoning of Spirit whose reasoning affords organic understanding and wisdom not just mere perception.

2 Corinthians 7:10 (KJV): For godly sorrow works repentance to salvation not to be repented of: but the sorrow of the world works death.

WHAT IS MAN?

Romans 2:4: Or despise thou the riches of his goodness and forbearance and longsuffering; not knowing that the goodness of God leads thee to repentance?

2 Timothy 2:25: In meekness instructing those that oppose themselves; if God peradventure will give them repentance to the acknowledging of the truth;

Hebrews 12:17: For ye know how that afterward, when he would have inherited the blessing, he was rejected: for he found no place of repentance, though he sought it carefully with tears.

Isaiah 1:18: Come now, and let us reason together, saith YHWH: though your sins are as scarlet, they shall be as white as snow; though they be red like crimson, they shall be as wool.

Genesis 4:10: YHWH said, "What have you done? The voice of your brother's [innocent] blood is crying out to Me from the ground [for justice]. 11: And now you are cursed from the ground, which has opened its mouth to receive your brother's [shed] blood from your hand.

Since the original transgression of man against the word and law of *YHWH*, sin entered into the world and a sin nature was passed along to the seed of Adam after him. No one has to teach you to do wrong, it is in you from inception. Why is this so? Because that act of disobedience and separation from YHWH came on a spiritual level because YHWH is Spirit and the spirit of the enemy filled the void of that separation. Until you are born again of the water and the Spirit and accept the atonement that has been made on your behalf, there is no capability to repent from sin or to gain deliverance from its effects and consequences.

Without the shedding of blood there is no remission (cutting it back reducing the effect) of sin. The blood of The Anointed Yahshuah saves and the Word of *Yahweh* (the bread of life) heals the mind because the mind was the first thing affected causing wrong perception when our forefathers ate of the tree of the knowledge of good and evil. This is what is symbolized in Holy Communion (one common union). The bread and the wine are concepts representing substance and form. We are what we eat, so bread is a mental concept that represents sustenance for life and His blood is the life force that carries identity as DNA, so "the power of life is in the blood." His righteous blood (as opposed to the contaminated blood of Adam) atones for sin and relates us in identity to our divine nature. This is the picture of Holy Communion Matthew 26:26 Yahshuah took bread blessed and broke it and gave to them and said, "take eat; this is my body". I need to point out two things about this picture, one is that man ate something (fruit) in disobedience and it caused them to sin being issued the penalty of death. Man could not eat from the tree of life, but he must eat something to rectify his death problem. No problem, Christ gave them the bread of life that came down from heaven. Two, He broke the bread that symbolized his body because out of One comes the two again just like in the beginning (One Yah whose "image" is Male and Female). One bread broken and divided in two, and then distributed amongst the disciples to eat. Two bodies are given by Yah (Yahshuah & Christ) the one a natural body that became the sacrifice for sin and the other that body resurrected and glorified. One body was given for them while the other body was given to them. Holy communion is a transferal of life (re-union over separation) and an exchange of eternal life for eternal death. What of the wine that symbolized the blood? Glad you asked. One significant thing about blood is that it carries white cells that fight off infections and disease and red cells that carry oxygen and nutrients that sustain life. His blood that was shed for us fights the disease and infection of the sin nature as well as gives us spiritual life, or in another word eternal life. Adam and Eve did not originate sin, Satan did. They just activated it allowing it to enter into the world, passed it on through race suggestion and Christ the last Adam came to rectify the problem. This is what Paul explained in his epistle to the Church at Rome.

Romans 5: 12: Wherefore, as by one man sin entered into the world, and death by sin; and so death passed upon all men, for that all have sinned: 13: (For until the law sin was in the world: but sin is not imputed when there is no law. 14: Nevertheless death reigned from Adam to Moses, even over them that had not sinned after the similitude of Adam's transgression, who is the figure of him that was to come. 15: But not as the offence, so also is the free gift. For if through the offence of one many be dead, much more the grace of G-d, and the gift by grace, which is by one man, Yahshuah the Messiah, hath abounded unto many. 16: And not as it was by one that sinned, so is the gift: for the judgment was by one to condemnation, but the free gift is of many offences unto justification. 17: For if by one man's offence death reigned by one; much more they which receive abundance of grace and of the gift of righteousness shall reign in life by one, Yahshuah The Messiah.) 18: Therefore as by the offence of one judgment came upon all men to condemnation; even so by the righteousness of one the free gift came upon all men unto justification of life.

Also, in this same letter to the Church at Rome, Paul talks about the power of the carnal nature or sin nature (the seed of the serpent) that is at war with the Spirit of *YHWH* and at enmity with the woman (feminine soul principle of man's being). You may recognize how I keep shifting the focus back to us as individuals and off of the biblical characters who are only presented throughout the Bible to provide a self-portrait or mirror to look at. It is important that you know that so you can get the full benefit out of this mandate.

Romans 7:14: For we know that the law is spiritual: but I am carnal, sold under sin. 15: For that which I do I allow not: for what I would, that do I not; but what I hate, that do I. 16: If then I do that which I would not, I consent unto the law that it is good. 17: Now then it is no more I that do it, but sin that dwells in me. 18: For I know that in me (that is, in my flesh,) dwells no good thing: for to will is present with me; but how to perform that which is good I find not. 19: For the good that I would I do not: but the evil which I would not, that I do. 20: Now if I do that I would not, it is no more I that do it, but sin that dwells in me. 21: I find then a law, that, when I would do good, evil is present with me. 22: For I delight in the law of G-d after the inward man: 23: But I see another law in my members, warring against the law of my mind, and bringing me into captivity to the law of sin

*which is in my members. 24: O wretched man that I am! Who shall
deliver me from the body of this death?*

*1 John 3:4: Whoever commits sin transgresses also the law: for sin is
the transgression of the law.*

Sin is the only thing that can separate and disintegrate the
relationship between man and his source of life. This is why it
logically leads to the ultimate separation called death. Sin is first an
internal separation of the mind, will, and emotion. When you
transgress your own conscious or go against how you feel then you
are divided and not whole within yourself. *YHWH*, the Self
Originating and Self Existing One is Spirit and Life to all. The
Messiah declared of His own self, "I Am the Way, Truth, and the Life,
and no man comes to the Father but by me" (St. John 14:6). This may
seem narrow and dogmatic to some; however, it is a statement of
absolute truth. To transgress or to go against life is to go toward
death. To go against the way, you must go toward the detour; to go
against the truth, you must go toward the lie. *Yahshuah* demonstrated
oneness with *YHWH* and always revealed that *YHWH* was the source
of His words and miraculous works. He said, "I and the Father are
one." One in thought, one in action, and one in Spirit. We all must
come to the Father in the same manner that *Yahshuah* did, through
the Spirit of Christ. Christ is the incorruptible, impregnable seed of
Yahweh that is the very nature of *YHWH* in man. Sin is separation or
death from the very essence of life Himself.

Let's examine the list of the words for sin from the Hebrew
writings and the New Testament Greek writings.

Hebrew words from Scripture on sin are:

1. Chata – means to miss the mark. If you shot an arrow poorly you not only miss the target, you hit something you were not supposed to hit causing damage elsewhere.

2. Ra – means breaking up or ruin. It indicates something both morally wrong and damaging. It is translated as "wicked."

3. Pasha – means rebel and is translated as transgression.

4. Awon – means iniquity and guilt.

5. Shagag – means to err or go astray as a lost animal or a child in a store. The one who went astray was ignorant but still responsible to truth.

6. Asham – means guilt before God and is associated with the tabernacle.

7. Rasha – means wicked, the opposite of righteous.

8. Taah – means to deliberately, not accidentally, wander away.

Greek words from Scripture for sin are:

1. Kakos – means bad as in morally bad.

2. Poneros – means evil and usually moral evil. Often used to describe Satan and demons.

3. Asebes – means godless or ungodly.

4. Enochos – means guilty and when used legally it usually refers to being worthy of capital punishment.

5. Hamartia – means to miss the mark.

6. Adikia – used to refer to any unrighteous conduct.

7. Anomos – means lawless and is translated "iniquity."

8. Parabates – means transgressor and refers to violations of the law.

9. Agnoein – refers to ignorant worship.

10. Planao – means to go astray and is used of leading or deceiving others or self.

11. Paraptoma – means falling away and usually, intentional falling away.

12. Hypocrisis – translated "Hypocrite" and refers to: People who interpret falsely, people who pretend like an actor, and people who follow false interpretations that are known to be false.

The prophet Isaiah spoke to the nation of Israel about the condition that they were in because of their iniquity and transgressions.

Isaiah 1:4: Ah sinful nation, a people laden with iniquity, a seed of evildoers, children that are corrupters: they have forsaken the Lord, they have provoked the Holy One of Israel unto anger, and they are gone away backward. 5: Why should ye be stricken anymore? ye will revolt more and more: the whole head is sick, and the whole heart faint.6 From the sole of the foot even unto the head there is no soundness in it; but wounds, and bruises, and putrefying sores: they have not been closed, neither bound up, neither mollified with ointment.

Isaiah 55:7: Let the wicked person abandon his way and the evil person his thoughts; let him return to Adonai, and he will have mercy on him; let him return to our Elohim, for he will freely forgive. 8: "For my thoughts are not your thoughts, and your ways are not my ways," says Adonai. 9: "As high as the sky is above the earth are my ways higher than your ways, and my thoughts than your thoughts."

Isaiah 59:2: But your iniquities have separated between you and your G-d, and your sins have hid his face from you, that he will not hear.

Christ is the wisdom and power of *Yah* that dwells inside a believer and we are complete only in Christ. The Bible points out to us that a double-minded man is unstable in all his ways and cannot receive anything from Yah. We must ask for wisdom and He will give it to us so that we may have confidence and certainty. Be singular in your vision, your real sight is the inner vision which is the light of the mind. Some traditions talk of clairvoyance, the third eye, the opening of the pituitary and pineal glands, the crown chakra, and so forth. They all allude to the fact that one must have a greater vision than just the 20/20 vision of the material plane. There was a time when the extra sensory perception was the norm for mankind, when the Yah-nature was at strength in man and not the sin nature.

All these religious practices, whether pagan or Christian that involve awakening something within or ascending the lower nature, are unnecessary to the regenerated Man. The Christ within can and will restore the soul of man to its oneness with the omniscient One. The task is, it must hit a critical mass (eight percent of the total population) to make an effect on the human record of the soul that we call collective consciousness. That is a new age term yet there is nothing new under the sun. The power of agreement is what Nimrod used to unify the people in the plain of Shinar in building the Tower of Babel (Genesis 11:1-9).

Let me go back to the point of unity and restoration through Christ hitting a critical mass and why this is important for the restoration of mankind. Though it will not happen until the millennial reign of the Messiah (Revelation 20:6), it will affect all the earth. And as easy as it is to do evil now, it will be to do right then. The polar shift or pendulum swing will be reversed between good and evil, light and darkness, and man will be restored to his inner sight.

Psalm 23:3: He restores my soul: he leads me in the paths of righteousness for his name's sake.

He restores my soul (your character, fixed image, identity, personality). Christ restores our soul to a complete and integrated whole. The word integrate means to complete or make one. Trauma splinters and takes apart the heart with pain and fear. Christ will mend the broken heart, take away the pain and fear, and give liberty to the captives of sin. Transformation is gradually happening at the present for individual believers and for mankind as a whole. Restoration and transformation are the whole reason Christ was made manifest in the world. Romans 12:2: "Don't be conformed to this cosmos but be transformed by the renewing of your mind." The word renew according to this Bible context means to bring back to wholeness. We will come back to the singular mind (*Yah's* image) we were created with from the beginning, before the soul dividing tree of the knowledge of "good and evil" separated man from his origination.

Man is a tripartite being, three parts of one whole: Spirit, Soul, and Body. We discussed this in a mandate above but let us look at it now from a Christ-centered position.

Theanthropos (Yah-Man) *Yahshuah*: The Christ = Perfected Man. He was made lower than the angels for the suffering of death's sake but through resurrection was given a name (authority) above every name, subjecting all authority in Heaven and Earth under him.

Theos is Greek for God and anthropos is Greek for Man so the theanthropos is God-Man, referring to *Yahshuah* the Christ. Another word that describes the union of the Spirit and matter as it relates to Man is hypostatic. This word means a state of union between two substances, (true being: entity, essence, substance), or natures in one unified person. The Westminster Confession describes the hypostatic union this way, "The Redeemer of God's elect is the Lord Jesus Christ, who being the eternal Son of God became Man, and so was and continues to be God and man in two distinct natures and one person, forever."

Let me summarize in a few statements the state of affairs. Righteous angels and fallen angels (who are now largely demons) outrank man (Psalm 8:4-5) and can influence or possess (if disembodied) everything lower than themselves; yet, Yahweh crowned Man king on earth. The devil usurped authority from Man and Christ won it back. Christ rose from the dead and is lifted above all ranks of powers, thrones, rulers, dominions, and all authority in heaven and on Earth is His. We are now converging on the point of this whole book. Man, through his identity in Christ, is restored to his rightful place as was *YHWH's* purpose before the formation of the world. Man's redemption through Christ is to gain Yah-nature to receive everlasting eternal life. You can't get perfection from something less than perfect. Christ is a perfect union of the Spirit and matter dwelling omnipresent under the direction of omniscience infused with omnipotence. We are to be brought into this perfect union through Christ. "Therefore, if any man be in Christ, He is a new creation" (2 Corinthians 5:17).

Christ is a position of authority not a name; it is a rank in file position. Apostles, Prophets, Evangelist, Pastors, and Teachers all file in rank under Christ (The Anointed One) to bring the family of believers to a union and the full understanding of Yah nature through Christ.

Ephesians 4:13: Till we all come in the unity of the faith, and of the knowledge of the Son of God, unto a perfect man, unto the measure of the stature of the fullness of Christ.

Psalm 8:4-94: What is man, that thou art mindful of him? and the son of man, that thou visits him? 5: For thou hast made him a little lower than the angels, and hast crowned him with glory and honour. 6: Thou made him to have dominion over the works of thy hands; thou hast put all things under his feet: 7: All sheep and oxen, yea, and the beasts of the field; 8: The fowl of the air, and the fish of the sea, and whatsoever passes through the paths of the seas. 9: O Lord our Lord, how excellent is thy name in all the earth.

Hebrews 2:6-11: But one in a certain place testified, saying, What is man, that thou art mindful of him? Or the son of man that thou visits him? 7: Thou made him a little lower than the angels; thou crowned him with glory and honor, and didst set him over the works of thy hands: 8: Thou hast put all things in subjection under his feet. For in that he put all in subjection under him, he left nothing that is not put under him. But now we see not yet all things put under him. 9: But we see Yahusha, who was made a little lower than the angels for the suffering of death, crowned with glory and honor; that he by the grace of G-d should taste death for every man. 10: For it became him, for whom are all things, and by whom are all things, in bringing many sons unto glory, to make the captain of their salvation perfect through sufferings. 11: For both he that sanctifies and they who are sanctified are all of one: for which cause he is not ashamed to call them brethren.

1 Corinthians 15:27: For he hath put all things under his feet. But when he saith all things are put under him, it is manifest that he is excepted who put all things under him. 28: And when all things shall be subdued unto him, then shall the Son also himself be subject unto him that put all things under him, that YHWH may be all in all.

Ephesians 1:19-23: And what is the exceeding greatness of His power to us-ward who believe, according to the working of his mighty power, 20: Which he wrought in Christ, when he raised him from the dead, and set him at his own right hand in the heavenly places, 21: Far above all principality, and power, and might, and dominion, and every name that is named, not only in this world, but also in that which is to come: 22: And hath put all things under his feet, and gave him to be the head over all things to the church, 23: Which is his body, the fullness of him that fills all in all.

Hebrews 2:8: Thou hast put all things in subjection under his feet. For in that he put all in subjection under him, he left nothing that is not put under him. But now we see not yet all things put under him.

He promised the believer the same resurrection power and new life of authority therefore, He has quickened us together in Christ. If any Man be in Christ, he is a new creature and has no condemnation. Dominion is restored to man through the Yah-Man. The un-regenerated Man is still bound under principalities and powers that govern this present evil world.

2 Corinthians 4:3-4: But if our gospel be hid, it is hid to them that are lost: 4: In whom the god of this world hath blinded the minds of them which believe not, lest the light of the glorious gospel of Christ, who is the image of God, should shine unto them.

Colossians 2:8-10: Beware lest any man spoil you through philosophy and vain deceit, after the tradition of men, after the rudiments of the world, and not after Christ. 9: For in him dwells all the fullness of the Godhead bodily. 10: And ye are complete in him, which is the head of all principality and power:

Though the stars which were created for signs and seasons tell a great deal about our birth path and soul tendencies, they fall far short of telling us our purpose and destiny. The zodiac was never intended to lead man to his destiny. It, just like the law and commandments, was an ordinance of the angels and governs the earth until man masters himself through Christ and is born of the Spirit.

Galatians 3:19: Wherefore then serve the law? It was added because of transgressions, till the seed should come to whom the promise was made; and it was ordained by angels in the hand of a mediator.

Job 38:33 Knowest thou the ordinances of heaven? canst thou set the dominion thereof in the earth? Jeremiah 31:35, Colossians 2:20 these scriptures speak in concert with Job 38:33

We have been made higher than the celestial realm so astral projection, the Akashic record, remote viewing and all the like can never help man reach the ultimate, which is union with the mind of Christ.

The next human evolution is Christhood, It will be inspired by the Holy Spirit not technology or in some cases tricknology. Contrary to secular humanist, no matter how advanced things seem, it can never lead to a true utopia if it is inspired by the un-regenerated mind of man. This new age (which is not new at all) of science and medicine will have us think that age defying biochemical breakthroughs, plastic surgeries, androids, Artificial Intelligence, genetic cloning, or modifying and bioengineering is our answer to everlasting life. I will venture to say that all those artificial means of forcing evolution will only lead to further disintegration and separation from the source of life. The Creator has already predestined us to evolve through Christ before He laid the foundation of the world. Sin and disobedience were all factored into the equation. Remember that He is eternal and outside of this space-time continuum that we are temporarily passing through. He is the beginning and the end of all things.

Let me share some insights about the Godhead we call a Triunity: Father, Son, and Holy Spirit. *YHWH* is in Christ via the Spirit (the Medium) making them One. The Anointed Son is the glory of the Father and the Holy Spirit is the glory of the Anointed Son—meaning only the Son can reveal the Father and only the Spirit can reveal the Son who reveals the Father. The anointed Messiah, Son of the living Yah, is the Yah-Man that we must be baptized into and resurrected as. We are to be conformed to the image of His dear Son. The Holy Spirit that once hovered over the face of the deep is now dwelling in the hearts and minds of those who have accepted Christ, the light of truth. He is revealing and manifesting a new Heaven and a new Earth. We are citizens of the New Yerusalem which is coming down to us from Heaven or the Christ mind in us. Remember Christ taught that the kingdom of Heaven is within. It does not come with observation. Once He changes our mind, will, and emotion into His very own, a new Heaven and a new Earth is the only thing that can result. (Revelations 21: 1-7).

Luke 17:20-21: And when he was demanded of the Pharisees, when the kingdom of YHWH should come, he answered them and said, The kingdom of G-d cometh not with observation: 21: Neither shall they say, Lo here! or, lo there! for, behold, the kingdom of God is within you.

Matthew 6:22: The light of the body is the eye: if therefore thine eye be single, thy whole body shall be full of light.

Tikkun is a Hebrew word meaning to fix or to rectify; it has several connotations which imply repairing, restoring, or mending. *Tikkun Olam* or mending the world is a term made known by Rabbi Isaac Luria referring to a world that was made void and a world set in formation and order. I would like to borrow this Hebrew word to say that man needs *Tikkun Nefesh* or the mending of his soul. The darkness and voids that sin leaves the soul in is the only thing that hinders man from knowing his full identity.

The soul must be made whole and not remain fragmented or fractured. The broken heart must be mended and made whole again. This is exactly what the man-child born of the womb-man, Eve, came to do.

John 7:38: He that believeth on me, as the scripture hath said, out of his belly shall flow rivers of living water.

The heart is the door that the Spirit must come through to commune with you as a being of mind, will, and emotions. The navel of your belly connected you in the womb to both the spirit world and the earth as you were suspended between the two. The belly is referring to the place in which that connection is housed. So, this reference to the navel is symbolic and signifies that from the place unifying the spirit and the material aspect of your being is where the living essence of life will spring up and keep springing up to eternal life. It is the fountain that never runs dry, the drink that is in you and will never allow thirst.

Revelation 3:20: Behold, I stand at the door, and knock: if any man hears my voice, and opens the door, I will come in to him, and will sup with him, and he with me.

As I conclude, the question this book puts forth is what is Man not what was Man. As in the beginning, Man was created in the likeness and image of *YHWH*. So, Man is the image or mirror reflection of *YHWH*. Sin fractured that image and like a broken or shattered mirror can only produce fractured images and not the whole picture, so we as a sinful Man can only reproduce a fractured image of the Divine. Sin produces another mentality which creates a different personality. The shame and guilt that comes with doing wrong makes one attempt to hide their behavior from potential observers. It also makes one try to justify and give rationality first to self then to others. As a coping mechanism, we splinter ourselves into the person who enjoys the pleasure of the wrong and dislikes the nagging of their own conscious. We have become the person who feels guilty and wishes to rectify the wrongdoing that has become habitual.

If sin is missing the mark and falling short of the glory of *Yahweh*, then doing the right thing or being righteous is hitting the mark and standing in the glory of *Yahweh*. So, we must ask: What is the mark and how do we define the glory of Yahweh? The mark is Divine likeness and the glory of Yahweh is the ability to reflect His image. When we fall short of that because of sin and disobedience, it is hard for us to face ourselves in the mirror. A famous singer wrote a song that speaks to this fact. He said, "I'm starting with the man in the mirror and I'm asking him to change his ways. If you want to make the world a better place, take a look at yourself and make a change."

I don't know Michael Jackson's spiritual status, yet he was speaking a biblical truth. If you want to look at that from a purely spiritual point of view you can correctly say take a look at your divine self and make a change (align to that image). The Word of *YHWH* is the mirror for the soul of man. How we align mentally and emotionally with the Word lets us know if we are reflecting the image of *Yahweh* or not. The Word is used by *YHWH* to heal us emotionally and deliver us mentally from the destruction of His Divine image (reflection of His image), which is what makes Man who and what he is. Man is the reflective image of his and her Divine Creator.

James 1:22-24: But be ye doers of the word, and not hearers only, deceiving your own selves. 23: For if any be a hearer of the word, and not a doer, he is like unto a man beholding his natural face in a glass: 24: For he beholds himself, and goes his way, and straightway forgets what manner of man he was.

If you just read the Word, hear it taught, and agree with its truth but don't practice it as a lifestyle you will never be consistent in reflecting the image of *YHWH*. Without exercising the principles of the Word daily, you will come across trials and tribulations that will dominate your carnal mind because you are untrained in the Word and unskilled in spiritual warfare. This will cause you to miss the mark and fall short of the glory of *YHWH* every time.

The true self of man that transcends personality and material makeup is the likeness and image of *YHWH*. Sin separates an individual from reproducing the true self in his personal character. If sin goes unchecked, it will lead to an ultimate destruction and separation from the divine self (Lake of Fire).

Think of an actual mirror. If the one standing in front of the mirror moves behind the mirror they don't leave the room, yet the mirror can no longer reflect what is not there in front of it. Conversely, if the mirror shatters and all the small pieces were then crushed it will cease reflecting anything. The Omnipresent life force is always there but His eyes are purer than to look at evil.

He says at certain places in Scripture, "I hid me." On the other hand, souls get so tainted in sin that there is no repentance in the heart and the mind grows reprobate. That is equivalent to the shattered mirror that is crushed, losing its ability to reflect anything. That soul has lost itself. We say phrases that indicate this behavior, like, "You are getting beside yourself." Getting beside yourself as opposed to standing in unity with yourself." "You were just not yourself today." Your behavior indicates that yourself was not directing your actions. We are spirit beings and the Holy Spirit of *Yahweh* is the true nature of man reflecting the Divine law and the will of the Father. Hence, the Scripture teaches us to walk in the Spirit, so we won't fulfill the lust of our flesh. Every sin and break from the "True Self" is a fracture or line of division from the image of the true self like the lines in a shattered mirror.

The remedy for a creation that has fallen in sin and shattered as a mirror, is Christ the Anointed Son of *YHWH*. Christ is the perfect reproduction of the image of the Father. We are to be conformed to the image of His dear Son who is His unbroken, unblemished mirror reflection.

Yahshuah understood this and that is why He could say to His disciple who asked him to, "show us" The Father, "Have I been with you all this time and you have not seen the Father, I and my Father are one." In other words, I am a picture of the invisible *YHWH* in action. He said, "I do nothing except I hear and see Him do it first." I echo and mirror the Heavenly Father.

1 Corinthians 13:12: For now we see through a glass, darkly; but then face to face: now I know in part; but then I shall know even as also I am known.

We are constantly growing into the full image of Christ–stage by stage, from faith to faith and from glory to glory until we redeem our identity as Man.

1 Corinthians 11:7: For a man indeed ought not to cover his head, forasmuch as he is the image and glory of God: but the woman is the glory of the man.

The word glory here can be defined as the reflection of. After the fall, Yahweh told the woman your desire will be to dominate your mate, but he shall rule over you. This is not as negative towards women as it seems for the Scripture says that the wife is the crown of her husband. If we look at it metaphorically, the glory of the woman (soul) is the body (man; its outer expression).

2 Corinthians 4:4: In whom the god of this world hath blinded the minds of them which believe not, lest the light of the glorious gospel of Christ, who is the image of YHWH, should shine unto them.

The problem with the world is that men are blinded from their true identity in Christ as the image of Yahweh. Your self-portrait determines your actions and beliefs which in turn determines your consequences and results. As a man thinks in his heart, so he is.

Colossians 1:15: Who is the image of the invisible God, the firstborn of every creature.

This Scripture speaks of Christ as the first born of every creature; He is the first in a new order or a new creation through resurrection from the dead, which implies there is more to follow. There are many Scriptures that confirm this truth.

One may ask: How do we deal with the sin nature until the full transformation of our soul takes place? When you pour a gallon of clean water into a small cup of dirty water, it will overflow and make the dirty water disappear. It's not that all traces of dirt are actually gone but it is so diluted that it is not apparent. So it is, when we are continuously filled with the living Word. The Spirit of *YHWH* will baptize us, spring up in us, and fill us to the point that our sin nature may be submerged and hardly noticed. I believe that is the implication of the often-used word "saints"referring to the children of the I Am.

When the regenerated soul and body of man is glorified (fully reflecting the image of *YHWH*) sin and separation will never again be a factor.

Just as a snowman is a Man made of snow or snow made to reflect the image of a man, The Yah-Man is a man made of Yahweh or man made to reflect the image of Yahweh. Yahweh is Spirit so the Yah-Man is one in essence with Yah as Spirit. It is the Spirit that is in us that determines what we are in essence. We hear terms such as the spirit of the world, evil spirit, Spirit of truth, etc. David said renew in me a right spirit, create in me a clean heart after he did evil deeds and was convicted by the truth. *Yahweh* puts His Spirit in us and is writing His word on the tables of our heart and mind (feeling and thinking). Being filled with and walking in the Spirit of *YHWH* is the only way that we will be what Man is created to be. The inner man is another word the Scripture uses to describe the *Yah's* nature as it tells us to be built up in the inner man. The Spirit is willing, but the flesh is weak when it comes to doing things that require faith in the word of Yah. We must build ourselves up on our most holy faith praying in the Holy Ghost.

Ephesians 3:16: That he would grant you, according to the riches of his glory, to be strengthened with might by his Spirit in the inner man; 17: That Christ may dwell in your hearts by faith; that ye, being rooted and grounded in love, 18: May be able to comprehend with all saints what is the breadth, and length, and depth, and height; 19: And to know the love of Christ, which passes knowledge, that ye might be filled with all the fullness of G-d. 20: Now unto him that is able to do exceeding abundantly above all that we ask or think, according to the power that works in us,21 Unto him be glory in the church by Christ Jesus throughout all ages, world without end. Amen.

Jude 1:20-24: But ye, beloved, building up yourselves on your most holy faith, praying in the Holy Ghost, 24: Now unto him that is able to keep you from falling, and to present you faultless before the presence of his glory with exceeding joy.

NOTES

NOTES

_____

_____

_____

_____

_____

_____

_____

_____

_____

_____

_____

CLOSING MANDATE

What is Man that *Yahweh* is mindful of him and the son of Man that Yahweh considers his ways? Man is the mirror reflection of The Invisible *Yahweh*. He is mindful of his offspring because it is how involution minds evolution or how thoughts monitor action to see if it lines up. The son of Man is the inheritance of *Yahweh* that will continue to evolve and revolve, manifesting the manifold wisdom and power endowed to him by his Creator.

We are the sons of *YHWH*–the Self Originating force of life and love producing joy, power, peace and beauty, which is our inheritance from the Heavenly Father. This is an inheritance that we can enjoy now and also in the ages to come for eternity, for it is the creative process that can be used to recreate to infinity. You and I are Man and we have a destiny prepared for us that eyes have not seen nor has ears heard, yet *YHWH* is revealing it to us by His Spirit within us. Stay tuned in to it, for it is your eternity.